FREEDOM TO CHANGE

Why You Are The Way You Are
And What You Can Do About It.

by
Gregory L. Little, Ed.D.
Kimberly J. Prachniak, M.S.
Stanley W. Prachniak, M.B.A.

Freedom To Change
Why You Are the Way You Are
and What You Can Do About It.

ISBN 10: 0-9655392-2-9
ISBN 13: 978-0-9655392-2-7

Freedom2Change.org
PO Box 9025
Memphis, TN 38190

www.freedom2change.org

ACKNOWLEDGEMENTS

This book is the result of years of collaborative work among the authors and represents an amalgam of ideas, concepts, and observations made over decades of practice in the helping professions. Theoretical ideas from Freud, Jung, Adler, Ellis, Skinner, and a vast range of others are found in this book. Thanks are expressed to our families, friends, and many colleagues, some of whom have passed away, for their support. Unless otherwise noted, photos are licensed from bigstockphoto.com.

DISCLAIMER: If you feel or believe that you need therapy, counseling, psychiatric help, or medical help, you should seek out these services from qualified providers. This book is *not* a substitute for professional help for emotional or psychological disorders. It is perhaps best described as a book that encourages self-help or what could be considered self-coaching. Self-coaching is an unusual term, but it implies managing one's life through an orderly process utilizing a plan and discipline. It also implies that you have the power to manage your own path through life. A series of workbooks, videos, and brief seminars are available for those seeking more support to implement the processes and concepts described in this book. In addition, our website provides free videos for individuals and life coaches who utilize these methods. Check our website for details: www.freedom2change.org.

We suggest that you read this book several times, picking it back up especially during times when you feel trapped in life or are struggling in relationships. This will allow the ideas in the book to sink in, marinate, and to even be viewed in a different light the next time you read it, depending on your circumstances at the time. You will get something different out of it each time you read it. You should also refer back to parts of it when you complete the Freedom2Change workbook exercises as they discuss concepts found here.

TABLE OF CONTENTS

PREFACE

How You Became You
and Our Purpose

There are three reasons that you are the way you are. First, you entered this world with a unique set of genetic characteristics and predispositions built into you. Depending on the particular personal characteristic you might consider, somewhere between 30% to 85% of what you are directly stems from your genetics (See Introduction to Psychology, 2017). Second, the environment and circumstances you were born into and exist within now have influenced the unfolding of your genetic predispositions and have greatly shaped what you believe about the world and your place in it. Third, you have made a series of choices that have led you to this exact place and precise moment of time. What you do right now can change things. That will continue to be true for you until your moments here run out. What you choose to do with this knowledge is up to you, which leads to our purpose for developing this material.

The primary purpose of this book is to remind you of your innate freedom. You can't do *anything* you want, and you can't become *anything* you desire, but you are capable of far more than you probably believe you are. You have the freedom to change almost anything.

Many people who read this book will be dealing with some personal issues. These issues may be relationship problems, work or career decisions, or any number of other possible personal conflicts. We want to remind you about an important truth you may already know, but it is probably buried deep within you and usually remains concealed from your awareness. It is this: *The major source of unhappiness and struggles in life come from trying to control things outside of our control while failing to control the things we can.* People devote too much time and energy lamenting what they don't have, while ignoring or neglecting what they do have and the things they *can* control. You have the freedom to believe whatever you want about this concept, but understand that there are consequences to all beliefs. In essence, becoming aware of the connection between control issues and happiness leads to genuine choices and living responsibly. If you stop trying to control things outside of your control, and focus on the things you do control, you can find your true path—the path that leads to genuine happiness. This is what Freedom to Change is about.

In addition, there are some basic guidelines and principles involved with how one can adequately manage the many control issues in life. How a person responds to these principles and guidelines is directly related to happiness, satisfaction, and what can be thought of as success in life. This book presents a summary of these basic guidelines. Again, you have the freedom to believe and accept these things as truth, or not. But the most important point here is that you really do have the freedom to change just about anything in your life, assuming you accept the control you do have and let go of anything you can't control. *However, you will change no matter what you do, and the world will change despite anything you try to do about it.* You can determine what the coming changes mean to you. The choice is yours.

Last, we need to say here at the beginning of this process and experience, that what follows isn't intended to be the "only" way. It is *a* way. What is here is an amalgam of ideas and truths from a vast array of knowledge. We have tried to present it in a simple format designed to give information, raise awareness, and lay out some of the basic choices that are commonly encountered in life. It presents a philosophy of living as well as practical suggestions and guidelines to find the truth about yourself, your life, and happiness.

CHAPTER 1

Life May Be Difficult, But It's Definitely Easier

Way back in 1978, author M. Scott Peck began his best-selling book, *The Road Less Traveled*, with the words, "Life is difficult." That's probably still true, but life has become a lot easier in a multitude of ways. Making life easier is one of the main motivators that drives innovation, invention, and advances in technology. No matter what you might believe about the beginnings of human life on Earth, from our very start, humans have consistently strived to make life easier for ourselves. Clothing, shelter, fire for warmth, containers for food and water, the evolution of hunting technology, the cultivation and preservation of food, and every other development you can think of has happened because we strive to make life easier, more predictable, and more controllable. We have come a long, long way as a species. And current technology is showing us that there is no end in sight to the trend of making things easier for ourselves.

Three Truths About Human Nature

There are three essential truths about human nature that we believe are necessary to reveal at the beginning of this process. All three of these human nature truths are programmed into us so strongly that we seldom comprehend their significance. Almost everything we do somehow relates to these three truths.

First, we have a primary objective built into our very nature. It is encoded into our brain and is the most fundamental drive of all. **It is the will to survive.** It is so powerful that we will do whatever is needed to survive—at all costs. Secondly, **survival of the species, or the**

overwhelming compulsion to reproduce, is deeply ingrained into us. The urge to engage in potential reproductive behavior is wired into us and is driven by chemical reactions in the brain and hormonal processes in the body. The feelings of attraction we have toward others are often directly related to potential reproduction. These reproductive urges are also directly linked to the will to survive. Sexual urges are driven by hormones produced at adolescence and these urges typically last throughout all of our adult life. Learning, your personal characteristics, and your stage in life all play a role in how these urges are handled, and inappropriate behavior can stem from not understanding or controlling such urges. Finally, we have a drive built into our genetic programming that ultimately serves the needs of the first two. It is **the drive to make life easier and more pleasurable.** An easier life makes survival more likely and also increases the likelihood of reproduction. Or so it might seem.

To succinctly restate these three truths, we are all programmed to survive, reproduce, and make our lives easier.

The extent of these three innate drives is so strong in us that few people truly comprehend how much of our behavior is motivated by them. For now, let's just consider the drive to make life easier. Think about the things you want for a moment. A new or better car might make your life easier. A new home, new clothes, and better gadgets can seem to make life easier. And at this moment, we stand at the edge of transformations in how we live that are so vast that they are nearly incomprehensible. These changes are already happening but will emerge with a swiftness not experienced before by any of us. Those below the age of 50 are not only likely to see a very different world than exists at the present moment—it's a virtual certainty. But even those of us older than 50 will experience vast changes. How you adapt or adjust to these changes, fight or embrace them, or try to ignore what's happening in your world is partly what this book is about. People are going to have a lot more of what we typically call "free time," and society will be faced with fundamental existential questions that call into question your very purpose for existence. If you have true awareness and the ability to analyze situations, you probably already sense that the decisions you'll face in the future will have profound significance. None of this is intended to elicit fear.

The intention is simple. You have the freedom to choose how you will respond to the brave new world that is rapidly approaching.

Freedom To Change

Freedom To Change describes the true power you possess which allows you to control your decisions and actions. It describes an optimistic essence of the human condition, which is often concealed by hopelessness, feelings of inadequacy, and despair. No matter where you are in life, you *can* change. You have choices—probably far more choices than you have ever realized. Maybe you feel trapped by life: trapped by a job; trapped in relationships; trapped by substance abuse; trapped by bills and other obligations; trapped by your past; trapped by a neighborhood; trapped by age; trapped by a body that is, perhaps, less than what you desire.

But you really aren't trapped because of those issues. You are trapped because of the beliefs you have formed in life and your actions in response to them. Over time, you have allowed the traps to form and you have remained within their confines for several reasons. But if you truly want to, you can attain freedom from those traps. You have the power to change almost anything in your life, if that's your desire. You have the freedom to change. You have power, and you have choices.

Sometimes our freedom is obscured because of other people and our circumstances, but more often we can't see the choices we have because we allow our beliefs to get in the way. We all have genuine limits, and the reality of the world surrounding us also imposes limits on each of us. There are limits present no matter where you are, no matter where you go, and no matter what you do. But you still have choices and you still have power in any given situation. And to cope with the changes that are soon coming to the way we live, you need to take control of as much power as you can. We say this at the beginning, because change is happening in society very quickly, so adjusting ourselves to the new realities is necessary to retain individual freedom.

Things Are Changing Fast

Almost everything in the world is evolving and changing rapidly. "Icons" in the media and politics are being exposed and falling, and this can all happen within a single day. How we engage in relationships, the words and terms that are considered to be appropriate or inappropriate, and our behavior within relationships are being revised so fast that many people are uneasy about their past and unsure about the future. But that's not all. What is heading our way is a revolutionary and unexpected way of life. And it'll all happen in a flash.

There will be more transitions in society and in the work world that no one can accurately predict. But some things are almost certain. Cash—physical money—will gradually disappear. Already, there are some businesses that no longer accept cash. Even physical credit cards will begin to disappear as more and more people use their devices to transmit payment information at checkout points. More and more "data breaches" will occur placing virtually everyone's identity and finances at risk. This has, by all definitions, already happened and will only worsen. Advances in technology will continue to cause dramatic changes and shifts in how the work world operates. How far this will go remains to be seen, but a lot of change is coming quickly. Soon, even more robotic workers and self-serve kiosks will replace many human workers. Banks will no longer have tellers and you'll interact only with a screen. But many people will never go to a bank. Fast-food employees will shrink in numbers dramatically because the need for cashiers and food preparers will diminish. The time is coming when you'll place your order, pay at an automated station, and the food will be delivered to you by a robotic device. Drones will make delivery of various types of goods faster, cheaper, and more efficient, reducing the need for delivery personnel. Bulk shipping will be done by self-driving trucks. Grocery stores have already launched online shopping and delivery to your home or vehicle, and more of that will soon be done by robotics. The use of automobiles is shifting as self-driving technology has arrived and many people are beginning to see that there may be no need for personal automobiles at all. It is thought that in roughly twenty years only fully-autonomous vehicles will be allowed on most public roads. Many of us already have automobiles with some self-driving capability. Even some construction work is already being done robotically. Entire homes, sans plumbing and electrical work, started being manufactured by huge 3-D *printers* in 2015. As this is being written, there are newer building technologies that assert that the electrical and plumbing components can be completed with 3-D printing technology.

Very soon you'll be able to have sex in a virtual world with anyone you wish. It will look, feel, and smell real. You'll be able to visit anywhere in the world or any place in a virtual reality and do whatever you wish, all from the comfort of a reclining chair. Information and misinformation is at our fingertips already. News and facts will become increasingly difficult to discern from ads and opinion. It will be even more difficult for people to distinguish what is real and what isn't. Society will splinter into smaller and smaller self-interest groups. This will be driven, in part, by the information that is collected through artificial intelligence (AI) software. Such software is used for marketing purposes to collect and analyze enormous amounts of data in order to accurately target products or services to consumers. The targeting of your interests shapes the content you see, ultimately narrowing your choices of goods, services, or stories to the ones that the "AI bots" think you are interested in the most. Instances of this can currently be seen in the ads displayed on web pages that you visit or in your social media feed. This same technology is used by a variety of special interest groups and others who seek your attention for one cause or another. Social media drives instantaneous change and will only increase in influence as our obsession with digital devices is enhanced to new levels. Rather than carrying devices with us, we'll eventually be directly "hot-wired" to them.

Countries will become increasingly diverse and the divisions in society will become even more apparent. Who knows where all this is going? The answer is partly that only the companies driving the rapidly evolving technology see where it is going, and even they aren't really in control. The truth is that technology has evolved to the point where it has begun to drive itself. The future is no longer predictable. We are in a world of change, more so than at any time in the recent past. All that is certain is that things will continue to change and will do so dramatically. Things no longer adjust and evolve gradually; they transition from one thing to another in a sheer moment. And you should expect more of this spontaneous flash-change. You have no real choice in controlling what will happen, but you do have real choices in how you respond to it. And you will respond, one way or another. Your response may be to do nothing, but that is still a response. It's up to you to make decisions based on what you believe and what you have done in the past, or to dig in and make some assessments that allow you to exert more control over your present and future life. In short, we are all being manipulated. And we are all manipulators. You can allow this change to sweep you along like a tsunami, or you can take conscious control of yourself and your life.

In this book we invite you to confront yourself and your world. It's something you need to do, because the alternative is to be left behind wondering about what could have been and wondering how you wound up in a life you didn't choose. Chances are that you already feel a bit left behind. But don't worry, the reality is that *everyone is always a bit "behind"* the sudden changes we are experiencing. No one is on top of—nor is anyone in front of—everything. Once you grasp that truth, you'll see that you have as much power over your life as anyone else has over his/her life. That leads us to this moment in time, a moment when you can decide how you'll adjust to the changing world. We invite you to reach deep inside yourself to discover the power you innately possess that will allow you to make changes and discover your true path in life. We'll present many possibilities to you, and in this process, you can pick whatever applies to you and do what you will with the rest. We'll tell you that there are some basic truths that are fundamental to living a happy and satisfying life. These are some of the same fundamental truths that have long been recognized. We'll tell you to be optimistic about your future, to be realistic about your present, and to keep in mind that you can change any or all of it. It's all about choice. And no matter what you consciously do, you will make a choice whether you want to or not.

CHAPTER

The Meaning of Life

One of us recently talked to a man who had just quit his job as a computer systems analyst. The man said that before he left on his last day, he asked his boss if he would be missed. His boss said something we've never heard before. He told him, "When you leave, you will leave a hole. The hole will be exactly like the hole your hand makes when you pull your hand out of a bucket of water." It was a stark mental image that led to mixed emotions.

After a few moments of silence, he was asked if that was an insult or if he had been viewed as a problem employee. He smiled and simply said, "No." He was liked by the others in the office and said he had been a good worker. He said in a matter-of-fact way, "that they would manage without him and adjust quickly." He had no discernible feeling about it at all.

More discussion led to the likely explanation. Everyone at his work site had the same underlying issue. All of them were doing a job that had no intrinsic meaning or significance—other than getting paid. The work paid well, but it wasn't personally important to them. They felt as if what they did really didn't matter in the bigger scheme of things. They weren't making much of a difference in the world. When he finds his "next" job, the man said that he expected the same type of work, with the same type of duties, but maybe at higher pay. He related that he was just a tiny, spinning cog in a complex, multi-cogged wheel that spun around whether he was there or not. If he left, another cog would replace him.

There is a common malaise in our modern world. People feel unimportant and insignificant. Unseen service people, conveyor belt manufacturing employees, packing and shipping workers, store clerks, construction workers, and fast food employees can all be in jobs that are repetitious and viewed as not having real significance. It's the same routine every day, seemingly an endless repetition of duties performed only for the pay. Few people are in a job they would happily do for free. There isn't much passion for *how* many of us are spending our work time. But it hasn't always been this way because people *had* to work to just survive and manage day-by-day. Remember that the primary directive we are born with is to survive.

The Not-So-Long-Ago Past

Once upon a time, around 100-200 years ago in the place where you are right now, there was no internet or Wi-Fi. There were no hardline phones, no cell phones, nor any electrical appliances at all. There were no automobiles or planes. People walked or traveled by horse if they were lucky enough to have one. The importance of horses can be grasped when you realize that people used to be hung for stealing them. The few stores in existence then were small, had little food, and were only located within towns or cities. Meat was salted and dried in strips to be preserved. All vegetables and fruits were either grown personally or bought from local sources, and were available only when they were in season. Most clothing was made by hand. Back then medical care was scarce, and the dental care was painful and primitive. Most toilets were in wooden outhouses with one or two holes in the ground. People used rags, plant husks, leaves, or whatever paper was handy for "wiping." Water often came from streams, springs, a well by the house, or if you were fortunate, from a hand pump. Many children died from diseases that are today considered as just a nuisance. Things like polluted water, infected tonsils, a simple cut, or a broken bone could kill you because antibiotics to treat such infections had not yet been developed. There were no ambulances nor emergency rooms. The average life expectancy was 30 to 40 years, and a third or so of the population died during childhood. It was a dangerous world. Survival was the dominant, driving force.

In that not-so-long-ago past, coal and wood were used for heating, cooking, and eventually to produce steam power. There was no air conditioning. There were no lightbulbs—candles or lamps that burned whale fat or kerosene were used for lighting. And all of those conditions were the reality only a few generations ago. It was like that for most rural Americans until the 1930s.

The steam engine was invented in 1803 and the first steam-powered "horseless carriage" came to America in 1863. Toilet paper became available in 1857. The first automobiles in America emerged around 1900 and the first airplane took flight about the same time. Things have really changed and the pace of change has accelerated, coming faster and faster.

Few people alive today remember these things, but chances are that your great-grandparents or their parents were there. The first author's grandparents drove a horse-drawn wagon through the mountains of Pennsylvania in the early 1900s selling products from what eventually became the *Great Atlantic & Pacific Tea Company*. It was how *A & P* began, which was once the largest retailer and a forerunner of massive grocery stores. They drove the wagon from farm to farm through rugged dirt roads in all sorts of weather. The people living in these areas looked forward to the convenience of having pots and pans, matches, coal oil, kerosene, canned food, salt, clothing, and other supplies brought to their door. Obviously things have changed, but we still like having things delivered to our doorsteps.

Tea wagon driven by Greg Little's grandparents.

In the 1800s and 1900s, the world saw dramatic changes. Who in the early 1800s could have foreseen something like the first 1888 *Sears & Roebuck* catalog where anything could be bought and delivered to your home or a nearby store? Sears & Roebuck eventually sold complete, ready-to-build houses, cars, motorcycles and virtually every commodity you could possibly need. In 1993 the Sears catalog became defunct and today, Sears is essentially a shell of what it once was. Who could have foreseen the rise of *Walmart* and the demise of small town centers that were once the hub of local commerce? And who would have guessed that even Walmart would eventually be challenged by the sudden appearance of online retail giants? If you carefully consider this, you can see how history has repeated itself. The former business giants didn't see the change coming and were behind the curve when it happened, leaving them at a disadvantage.

Few of you reading this remember how amazing it was when the first hand-held calculator was introduced back in 1970. You probably don't remember the first desktop computers in the late 1970s or how amazing the first desktop publishing computers were in the 1980s. For music and sound recordings, we have gone through rotating wax sound cylinders, vinyl records, reel-to-reel decks, cassettes, CDs, and now, to digital files. The same progression is true of video formats from reels to Beta, to VHS, to Laser Disc, to DVD, to Blu-ray, to digital. Cable television providers, once thought to be immune to market changes, never saw the alternatives coming that have forever transformed their business model. They all adapted by providing internet service and on-demand content, but that too will undoubtedly change. If you had the time and urge to do so, you could carry a digital file of every book ever published on a storage drive no larger than your little finger. And now we have the "cloud" to store all of our digital content. It appears that carrying a tiny thumb drive has become too much for us to bear. We want access to everything—everywhere and all the time, instantly. Libraries, once the hub of information for nearly everyone, have slowly been eroding into what can be seen as a type of museum or refuge for the downtrodden.

In the 1990s, the idea of a "self-driving" car was thought to be ridiculous and impossible by most people. But they already exist. How many of us just a couple years ago would have considered same-day delivery of products by remote-flying drones to be possible? More, much more change, is on the way. Life is very different today than it was just 50 years ago, or even only 5 years ago. If you can afford it, you can buy almost anything and have it brought to your doorstep. If you can't afford something, you can likely charge it or get a quick loan. A lot of people don't carry cash anymore and some people don't even carry credit cards. Instead, they pay using a fast swipe of a "phone" or other device. You can probably call anyone in the world from just about anywhere in the world using a tiny, hand-held computer that calls itself a smart phone. You can see the other person while you talk to him or her, and now, you can even do this on a tiny computer masquerading as a watch. Your phone talks to you, gives you directions, and answers questions. You can send out live video of yourself anytime and from just about anywhere. You can talk to a digital device in your home and have it order items for you, make reservations, answer questions, tell you what is on TV, tell jokes, and more. Today you can spend all your waking time in a "virtual" world where you can fight wars, kill countless people, steal cars, play games with sports stars, or have sex in this fantasy world—apparently without consequences. You can have immediate contact with "friends" anytime and from anywhere. Today, on average, you can count on living about 45 years longer than your great-grandparents. And you have a lot of "free" time. Even if you have the responsibilities of family and work, in comparison to the past, you still have spare time to fill. In short, the basic survival drive has declined a bit in influence because it has become much easier to survive. Survival, it seems, isn't what it used to be. But then, nothing is.

Before all of our "modern conveniences," people didn't have much spare time, and they tended to use all their energy just surviving from day to day. Their purpose of life was probably a bit simpler and much clearer to them. They had family obligations that involved survival: basic security, food, water, and shelter. They had to plan for the changing seasons, and whatever time was left was devoted to teaching their children and trying to make life a little better. Today, we have a lot more "spare" time. Most adults with jobs have about 70 hours of spare time each week. Of course, that time gets filled up with a number of responsibilities and tasks. Young people and those who don't work, or are retired, have even more "spare" time. How all that time is used has something to do with what each person sees as his or her purpose in life. To a great extent, "purpose in life" is what this book is all about.

Maslow's Hierarchy of Needs

Back in 1943, psychologist Abraham Maslow proposed that humans go through a series of growth stages, with each stage characterized by efforts to fulfill a set of underlying needs. This theory is based on the idea that this series of progressively important needs motivate humans at different points in life. It is astonishing how many theories have adapted the ideas Maslow put forth. Others who saw Maslow's ideas as valid and important presented his theory as a pyramid with the most basic needs at the bottom and then moving upward with more complexity at the higher stages. Maslow's theory is generally considered to have validity for individuals, organizations, and businesses. It is viewed as having genuine, practical application in the real world. And in the new world that is emerging in unexpected ways, these ideas carry even greater relevance to us.

Maslow's Hierarchy of Needs

Self-fulfillment needs

Psychological needs

Basic needs

Self-actualization: achieving one's full potential, including creative activities

Esteem needs: prestige and feeling of accomplishment

Belongingness and love needs: intimate relationships, family, friends

Safety needs: security, shelter, safety, financial stability

Physiological needs: food, water, warmth, rest

Survival and Safety

At the bottom of the pyramid, Maslow described the most basic needs that all humans strive to fulfill. These are basic survival issues: food, water, warmth, and rest. Just above those basics are safety needs such as shelter and security. Shelter, safety, and security usually include a sense of financial security and overall health.

It is believed that about a third of the world's population is stuck on these two lower levels, struggling on a daily basis to have food, water, and a place to live that hopefully provides basic security. They also struggle with health and financial issues. Modern, developed countries have a small portion of their populations struggling to meet these needs, but in general, *most* people in developed countries have the basic needs met.

One big issue with many people all over the world is how they meet the need for financial safety and health. That is, even though they seem to have met the basic needs, they live in fear of losing it all. That fear can be used as a tactic for manipulation. All kinds of insurance, various types of "coverage" on your car (the tires, electronics, maintenance, etc.), insurance in case you can't pay a credit card bill, coverage on appliances and so on, are sold on the basis of Maslow's lowest level: security. We aren't telling you to decline such offers; we are just making you aware that it's all about safety and security. We can be easily manipulated by those two very basic issues, and politicians and salespeople know it. But there are a lot of people who do live on the edge. Lots of people are at risk financially their entire lives, and they also struggle with health issues, which includes their level of health insurance coverage. A recent survey conducted by Careerbuilder.com (2017) found that almost 80 percent of Americans live paycheck to paycheck. The same survey revealed that 70 percent of workers are in serious debt and nearly 60 percent of us believe that we'll never get out of debt! What this all means, as it relates to Maslow's theory of needs, is that a lot of us are just keeping our heads above the water and believe that we'll always be struggling with the most basic level: survival & safety. According to Maslow, if this lowest level of needs isn't met, it is difficult to deal with the higher-level needs.

Belonging and Self-Esteem

Above the basic needs on Maslow's hierarchy are two types of psychological needs. The most fundamental of these is a *sense of belonging and love*. Relationships with friends, family, community, and co-workers are the critical components. Related to belonging and love is a need for *self-esteem*, a sense of worthiness and accomplishment along with feelings of *self-respect*. In the modern world, many people reach this stage and live their lives trying to maintain their self-esteem and self-worth. It's here where you find the most frequent difficulties in life: interactions with family, friends, co-workers, love relationships, and intimacy. *We need to be needed, and we seek to be important to others.* As people get older, these issues can be met by a ring of family and friends, but as people transition into their senior years, their circle of friends and family can, and will, shrink. Live long enough, and all of your friends will be gone. People come to feel less and less important and their self-esteem suffers. One's accomplishments in life can, and will, diminish in importance and relevance over time. There are many people who believe that we shouldn't dwell on the past—whether it was filled with accomplishments or not. Here is an example.

In 2003 the University of Alabama Press published a book entitled, *Ninety-Nine Iron* (by Wendell Givens). The book is about a college football team, which in 2012, was voted as the *Greatest Historic Football Team of All Time* by the College Football Hall of Fame. The school was a charter member of the Southeastern Conference. The team finished 12-0 and defeated all 12 opponents by an astonishing combined score of 322-10. Eleven of their victories were *shutouts* of the other team. Among others, they beat Tennessee, Texas, Georgia, Georgia Tech, Texas A & M, Mississippi, Auburn, and LSU, all of which were powerhouses at that time. Few people reading this will have ever heard of them, but it was the 1899 football team of *Sewanee, The University of the South*. In the middle of their season, *they played 5 road games in a span of only 6 days*, traveling thousands of miles by train to their games in Texas, Louisiana, and Mississippi. All of these road games were won by shutouts of the opposing teams. It was an almost incomprehensible accomplishment that will never be equaled. If you are a football fan, we know what you are thinking. Just bear with us for a few moments.

In the *Introduction* to his book, Givens related that he briefly visited the famous halfback and captain of the 1899 Sewanee team, Henry "Diddy" Seibels, in 1952. At that time, Givens was only gathering information for a newspaper article. Diddy Seibels was then a senior partner in an insurance agency and was described by Givens as quiet, friendly, and polite. Seibels handed Givens (the visiting reporter) a stack of printed information and then went back to work without reminiscing or talking about his team's achievements. Decades later, while writing his 2003 book, Givens lamented the fact that he hadn't taken any time with Seibels when he met him back in 1952. Givens did manage to speak with Seibels' two surviving sons, and they stated that their father didn't talk about his past glory and he often related to them that, "You shouldn't live on past glory" (p. 8). Givens' book also describes what the team members saw as their driving force. It was a sense of belonging to others, of being connected to something greater than one individual, a devotion to each other and devotion to a cause. In essence, it reflects exactly what Maslow described as our deep psychological needs: a sense of belonging and self-esteem.

Of course, the lesson in this isn't about football. It's partly about the passage of time, changes in everything, and relying upon or leaning on past glory and past achievements. The game of football has certainly changed dramatically. And the accomplishments of that 1899 team are today known by only a few people and will likely be demeaned by modern ideas and beliefs about football. Think about that for a moment.

If you are a football fan, you'll probably dismiss the accomplishments of that 1899 team because "the game has changed." Yes, it has. That is something that time does. Things change and the past gets diminished. Seibels and his other teammates went on to careers in other areas, including law and medicine, until they all, inevitably, passed on to become a footnote in college history. But they also showed that self-esteem and a sense of belonging doesn't end with accomplishing something or participating with others. It is a life-long pursuit that can go on to even higher levels. It's more about the underlying meaning of life and becoming something greater: striving to be something greater than we think we are. And that is what leads us to Maslow's highest levels.

Self-Actualization

At the top of Maslow's needs hierarchy is *Self-Actualization.* Self-actualization has formed the basis of countless human potential movements that began in the 1960s and continue to this day. Self-actualization is, at its core, a sense that one can become the best person that he or she can possibly be. It means that the individual has reached his or her full potential. It is a lofty goal. Later in his life, Maslow added a higher stage he referred to as *Self-Transcendence.* It is somewhat similar to the highest stage of morality that was proposed by psychologist Lawrence Kohlberg. It is a sense that there are universal principles of ethics based on the idea of fundamental justice and fairness. In essence, self-transcendence implies that the person has met all of the "lower" levels of need and has become more focused on the welfare of others.

While a lot of groups and programs focus on self-actualization and urge participants to become the best person they can be, many of these programs make some leaps past key issues. There are important parts of the process that should not be dismissed or overlooked. For many people, reaching their highest potential is not just difficult, but nearly impossible when their life's circumstances are taken into account. There are countless obstacles on the modern life path we all follow: bills, responsibilities of family, responsibilities of owning a home, health issues, limited opportunities for work, inflated costs of education, one's neighborhood, and aging—those are just a few things that can get in our way. Things change, and adjusting to all of the changes can consume nearly all of a person's time and effort.

People need a way to make intelligent adjustments and make the necessary changes when they encounter periods of transition and choice points. And they need a way to identify and address certain issues that have gotten them stuck in places they'd rather not be. They need to have an effective way to make choices and see how they will follow through with their choices. These are some of the things we hope to provide here. You need to have a way to organize things, evaluate them, make a realistic plan, and find the motivation to do what needs to be done. However, we aren't just talking about getting somewhere in life. Where you go in life matters, but what matters even more is *how* you get there.

What the last sentence of the prior paragraph means is that we not only want to provide some useful techniques and methods to change your life, but we want to suggest what we consider to be very basic and simple principles about *how* to live life. In brief, it means that we believe that with *most* issues and situations in life, there is a clear right and clear wrong. There are certain ways to live and behave that are not only more satisfying in the long run, but are also more just and correct choices. This assertion is one that a lot of human potential movements don't embrace or would rather ignore. They often assert that "right and wrong" don't exist. But we think that's a bit misguided. If you disagree with our assertion that "right and wrong" really do exist, then you are saying we are "wrong." Think about that.

Here is a simple example of our assertion that there are some basic ways to live that lead to better outcomes. A host of scientific studies, which we'll discuss later, show that happiness is linked to health. Positive, accepting emotions are linked to happiness and are also linked to being healthy. In addition, an emerging area called "positive psychology" asserts that there are certain behaviors and personal characteristics that lead to happiness. A few of those are developing healthy relationships, being mindful of the present, exercising, and so on. Even the famous billionaire Warren Buffet has weighed in on what we are calling "right and wrong." In his often-cited advice to young people (Elkins, 2017; Schwantes, 2018), he consistently relates that "honesty pays off" and that "being a good, decent person usually leads to success in business." Honesty can be asserted to be the most fundamental underpinning of happiness and success. In essence, our assertion is that being honest is usually the right decision. Developing healthy relationships, being mindful, and expressing positive emotions are usually the right choices. Warren Buffet has also frequently talked about finding your true purpose in the work you do. He has often stated, "When you go out in the world, look for the job you would take if you didn't need the money" (Mc-

Queeney, 2017). Sure, it's advice easily given, and often times it is difficult to follow. But it is still good advice. However, it doesn't answer the bigger questions: What is our purpose in life? Why do we exist?

There is an idea about our purpose in this life and sometimes it's expressed as doing what it takes to become the best you can be—taking into account all of your personal characteristics and abilities. In essence, it means living your life in ways that express what and who you truly are. We'll add to this the idea that there are situations presented to each of us every day allowing us to make choices that demonstrate the essence of our character. That is what self-actualization is all about.

What is the Meaning of Life?

Before we leave this chapter, we'd like to make a bold attempt to answer an important question. Perhaps more accurately, we want to foolishly try to answer it. It's a question we have all asked at one time or another: What is the meaning of life?

There are a lot of answers floating around. And many of them extend back to the dawn of human existence when our primitive ancestors looked into the night sky and wondered, "Why am I here, where did I come from, what is this all about?" Some self-help systems that are derived from self-actualization ideas will tell you there is no meaning at all to life. We are here because we are here, nothing more. "Life is a game," others say. One side says it's a game of "winners and losers" and they give you strategies and methods to compete with others so you can be one of the winners. Other approaches say life is more of a game like golf, a game you just play as best as you can—staying within the rules. Religious ideas about the meaning of life also abound, and depending on your preferred religion, life is about getting close to God or some higher power. Some say life's purpose is about doing God's will. Others say life is meant as a way to connect with a higher purpose or cosmic awareness. There are many other ideas, of course, including one that says life is just an evolutionary reality and it has no intrinsic meaning at all: We are alive until we aren't alive, and that's it.

We have a different answer. It's not necessarily the correct and only answer, but it's an idea that works. It is pragmatic. And it is simple. Here it is: *The meaning of life is whatever you make it to be. You determine your meaning of life.* You can make it religious, spiritual, a game, or anything else. It's up to you. For some people it's having power, money, sex, or just enjoying everything—having fun as long as you can. Others believe it's about their family, their religious beliefs, or following a particular cause. There are even people who see life's meaning as an ongoing struggle that only ends when they no longer exist. Whatever meaning you ascribe to life is up to you. It is your decision. We believe that there are some important principles and values successful people adhere to, but it's up to you to decide if they are true for you. We'll get to these ideas in later chapters. But you should understand that it's all up to you, and it has been that way for a long time.

If you could observe what a person does for an extended period of time, you would probably get an idea about what that person sees as his or her meaning in life. By seeing what that person does, you would get a glimpse of what that person values and believes, right? One example we have sadly observed is that some people seem to live as if the meaning of their life is to make it to retirement. They live day-by-day using a countdown, marking how many more years or days they have to work. They live day-by-day to make it to some imagined, better, future time and place. There are lots of other things we could mention. For example, let's imagine you observed what a hypothetical movie producer might have done for decades. Let's say you observed him making enormous amounts of money, wielding vast power over important business decisions that affect a lot of people, and regularly demanding—and forcing—sexual favors from prospective actresses for his films. Then you observe it all being denied—with him claiming that none of it ever happened. Assuming this person did all those abusive things, what would the meaning of life be for this person? We could go a lot further with this example, but the point is that no matter what a person says his or her meaning in life is, the genuine truth about it is shown by what the person consistently does. Of course, taking a snapshot of a specific time in a particular person's life wouldn't give a genuine and true picture of the person. There are different phases in life where some things fade in importance and others come to the forefront. That is partly what Maslow's theory is about. We progress through stages in life where some things fade in importance while others increase in importance. Think of it this way. When you were 8 years old, your meaning of life was different than it was when you turned 18. Chances are it'll be a lot different if you have kids. It'll change when you retire and probably change again when you reach age 90, and so on. But how you live your life reflects what you believe it's all about, at least at any particular moment in time.

Seeking to Be Something Greater Than We Are

We'll add one more important idea here. Over decades of working with all kinds of people, there is a conclusion we've reached about an underlying motive most people harbor deep within themselves. *We believe that most people seek to become something bigger and greater than they think they are at any given time.* Most people, at some point during their life, want to make a difference in the world. All of us are capable of being noble and doing the right thing. We want to be heroes, not martyrs. Everyone is capable of being noble and being redeemed. We don't want to just be ordinary. We all want to matter. The question of *how* we want to make a difference or matter is a critical point.

The noble motive and desire to become "something greater" can get twisted in some people until all that's left is the desire to be famous. Some mass killings, "spotlight seekers," and people doing outrageous things to get noticed are examples. YouTube contains rampant displays of people doing things in hopes of their video going viral. Consider the development of "reality television shows" creating people who are famous for just being famous and the effect that has had on modern culture. Ask high school age children what they want to be when they get older and the most frequent answer today is: "I want to be famous." They seldom say how they want to achieve the fame because it doesn't matter. Fame appears to be its own reward.

Back to Maslow

The real core of Maslow's theory is two-fold. The lower need levels are about safety, security, and procreation. In the modern world, these issues are typically dealt with by having a job, money, family, and relationships. There are lots of things a person can do to help ensure that safety, security, and procreation can be procured, including: getting an education, following a career path, developing skills, handling finances, and doing all the things necessary to attract beneficial relationships and then keep them. All of these things matter, however, it's important to recall the three facts about human nature that were related at the beginning of this chapter. We have fundamental drives built into us to survive, reproduce, and make life easier. All three of those drives are found at the lower levels of Maslow's hierarchy. The second and probably most relevant part of Maslow's theory comes after the basic needs are met.

In summary, what we want you to remember from this chapter are a couple key points. Everyone seeks out the basic needs of life: food, water, shelter, and security. There are some people who get stuck at this point by thinking they never have enough security (money and material objects). But most people in the modern world do achieve this basic level, and many of them didn't have to do much to achieve it. However, once these basic needs are met, people strive to meet several important psychological needs: developing meaningful and lasting relationships, and having a sense of self-worth. Finally, we seek to become something greater. Not many people get to that last part—but they want to.

CHAPTER

Two Simple Rules

While writing this book, a neighbor was talking to one of us. She was active in her neighborhood association by setting up a *Neighborhood Watch* and creating online venues for neighbors to express themselves and voice their concerns. On one of her neighborhood social media websites, there were postings and comments made by a wide range of people about crime, association issues, and various local events. Gradually, a few people became divisive and increasingly bitter. Many of their comments were highly political in nature and critical of anyone they thought disagreed with them. Some people complained if the neighbor deleted the most outrageous and vituperative comments, which was her prerogative as the site's administrator. For a time, the comments became increasingly bitter and she wrestled with the problem by trying to balance fairness, openness, freedom of speech, and other concerns she considered to be important values. People seemed to become more and more divided, precisely the opposite of her intentions. It caused a great deal of concern and became a frustrating issue that she struggled to confront. She wasn't sure what to do. What would you recommend she do?

First Rule of Decision-Making: Do No Harm

Those of us in the helping professions are taught a primary axiom derived from medicine. In a way, it's an established rule in all helping professions. There is a small bit of controversy in the medical community about it (Cooper, 2013; Hardy, 2006; Herbert & Sageman, 2008; Webster, 2017), but we'll stick to the simple and most common form. It's this: First, do no harm.

Do no harm. It's not always as easy to accomplish as it is to say. There are some in the helping professions who say "Do no harm" is a good idea to *always* aspire to, but it's not always clear in some situations. In most situations it is obvious what can cause harm, but certainly not in all circumstances. In therapy, counselors sometimes refrain from saying precisely what they may be thinking because they aren't certain how it may be received. What that implies is that the counselor isn't certain whether the patient might be helped or harmed by the potential comments. In reality, this happens all the time. For years the first author worked with a psychiatrist who was often unsure how to answer patients' questions about some medications that had been prescribed. But more relevant here are real life situations we face outside of medicine or counseling. For example, let's say you are a supervisor and a 10-year, model employee whom you really like and respect is not performing well at work. You suspect his work is being affected by his use of pain pills triggered by knee surgery in the last year. Since then, you have noticed his work ethic slowly slipping. He comes in late some days; his emails and letters often have careless errors in them; and he is not producing the amount of work that he should be during a typical day. You have asked him if everything is okay, told him that you have noticed these issues, and suggested he contact the Employee Assistance Program. He has only replied that everything is fine, that he knows he can do a better job, and he won't let you down. But his work has continued to decline over the last month, and you have noticed that some days, his speech is slower and he seems to move slower at work. How do you handle it?

He doesn't seem to want to face a possible pain pill addiction, and he is not taking any actions to improve his work. If you address his poor work in writing, it will go in his Human Resources file; you will then have to monitor his work in writing; and it could lead to him being fired. If he is fired, he will lose his family's health insurance and most likely will have trouble paying for counseling sessions. But if you do nothing and cover for him, it is not fair to your other employees who come in on time, work hard all day long, and end up having to do more work when that employee does not do his share. In addition, by not doing anything, you may be creating the opportunity for even more harm. Do you try and talk to him again? How long do you wait after this talk before you try something else? Will addressing his work in writing prompt him to seek the counseling that he needs? What if it doesn't? How do you "do no harm" in this situation? The truth is that life can be fraught with such dilemmas.

Life is complicated and some very, very problematic situations can emerge from the most unexpected situations. Every day we are faced with numerous decisions, big and small. You have probably been tempted by some events you have observed in real life. For example, should you say something if you see a parent screaming at a child and severely pulling the child's arm? Could your words somehow cause the parent to scold the child even more harshly later? Might your words do harm to the child or perhaps to you? There are endless other examples. Do you allow your children to watch television? How much time can they watch? Do they choose their shows? Do you let them spend time playing video games? Which games? What kind of food and drink do you choose for yourself and others? If you give some help to one person, does that deprive someone else? There are many more examples we could mention here, but you get the gist of how complicated things are. Nevertheless, we believe that "do no harm" is a great guiding principle for *everyone*, not just people in the helping professions. All of us have to figure out what that means for ourselves. *Using "do no harm" is a good starting point for making decisions*, but it's not quite enough.

The Second Rule: Do the Best You Can

While some people struggle with the first rule cited above, there is a seldom-mentioned second rule that can greatly assist decision-making in problem situations or when making choices. We aren't sure who said it first, but the first author has long taught it in college ethics' classes and in the training of treatment professionals. It is a way to encourage someone to do the best they can in a given circumstance. Theodore Roosevelt quoted one form of it in his 1913 autobiography. He mentioned Sq. Bill Widener as the source. Roosevelt's simple rule was: "Do what you can, with what you've got, where you are."

It means that we should aspire to *do the best we can with the re-sources available to us in any given situation.* Sometimes it means you might use a pen and paper to make notes at a time your preferred electronic device isn't handy. It might mean you allow your children to watch more television than usual at a time you need them to be preoccupied. Maybe it just means to smile and say a kind word to the parent engaged with a child. It can mean going to schools that are convenient and affordable, and seeking out a job that pays enough and is accessible to you. Where you live, what your background is, and who you know all come into play when making decisions like these. So you do the very best you can, using all the resources that are available to you, taking into account your location and situation. If what you really need is not available where you are, you can move if it is at all possible. In short, sometimes you have to go where the resources you need are available.

Doing the best you can, means just that. It doesn't imply perfection. Nor does it mean exhausting yourself. It doesn't mean changing everything, although that is something we'll discuss. It means looking at situations and circumstances, assessing them, doing a realistic evaluation of your beliefs, making informed choices, and then doing what you have chosen. If it doesn't work out, you repeat the process until you reach an acceptable outcome. But one thing that often gets in the way of a person doing the best he or she can, is that the person often focuses on what *isn't* available in a situation rather than dealing with what is actually there. Use the talents, knowledge, and tools that are immediately accessible to you to do the best you can *in that moment.*

Lamenting What Isn't

So many of us grieve what doesn't exist. We complain that we don't have the money, the time, or the looks to do something or get something, or attract someone we want. Lots of people look at others' lives and want what they have. We look at people born into money, people born with good looks, people who have good health, people who have good jobs, a good career, a good husband or wife, a nice house, a new car, or whatever. All of that yearning, lamenting, and wanting can only serve a useful purpose if it motivates you. One of the things we'll stress over and over is a simple fact about control. *There is one, and only one, thing you control in life. You can control what **you** do at any given time.* What you do in every moment of time has an effect on what situations you will face in the future. You can want all sorts of things in life, but it's up to you to do the things that'll lead you to them. You have the ability to make things happen *for you* and not let things happen *to you.*

You Are a Creation—Not Just a Compilation

In a very real way, who you are today, all of the things in your life right now, and what you do with your time, are consequences of everything you have done previously. In an imprecise way, each of our lives is a sort of compilation of events. But it's not all cause and effect. Nor is life just an accumulation of experiences. You, whatever the word "you" might mean at this moment, are a creation. You created yourself through a long series of choices, many of which you gave no real thought to when you made each choice. Nevertheless, many of us see ourselves as a sort of resume of experiences, accomplishments, and skills. We compile a list of our job experiences, our education, our skills, awards, and accomplishments. We present this list as a snapshot of who and what we are. Your snapshot is a necessary step in the process of applying for a job, and it summarizes some of the things you have done. But it doesn't accurately reveal who and what you are. So, who and what are you?

As was just stated, you are more of a *creation* than a compilation. Over your lifetime, you have created yourself from traits and abilities you were given, and the choices you made as you faced many opportunities and situations. Remember the second rule? *Do the best you can with the resources available to you in any given situation.* Every decision you have ever made either conformed to this rule or it didn't. Everything you believe about yourself and the world is a creation made from countless events you have experienced. It all came from continuous interactions among your innate qualities that were given to you from genetics combined with your learning experiences; watching, being around, and interacting with other people; and the choices and actions you took. In essence, you created yourself as you see yourself today. You created your sense of self—your identity. What this really means is that you have the ability to change it, if you really want to.

If you look at your life as just a compilation of events and memories, it keeps you stuck where you are—or stuck on the path you have created for yourself. Seeing yourself just as an accumulation of experience means that change has to be small and additive. If you choose to see it that way, you can. But a creation can change instantly. The neat thing about being a "creation" is that it can change fast through conscious decisions, either a little or a whole lot. A creation can transform into something completely different—up to a point, of course—if it chooses to do so. On the other hand, if you see your life only as a compilation, all you can do is stack something else onto the pile of accomplishments, experiences, and events in life. Understanding the freedom that comes from seeing life as a creation is a revelation. A creation can recreate itself instantly if it chooses to do so. At the very least, you can begin the process of recreating yourself at any time.

A Simple Example

There is a very good chance that you consistently dress in a certain way—your "style." Over time you have made choices about the type of clothing you wear, and the clothing you have accumulated in your dresser drawers and closets reflects those choices. Dressing in a particular way becomes a habit that is so ingrained into our behavior that most people are completely unaware of it. That is, the way you dress is largely an unconscious process. A different way to look at this is that over time you have gradually narrowed down your clothing choices to a set of styles you will wear for specific activities or for specific days of the week. You have limited your choices into a squeezed-down set of possibilities. Of course, this is both a necessary and appropriate thing to do. But rather than let this process occur through habit and unconscious processes, it's smart to make conscious and informed choices about the clothes you wear.

There is an old adage that is somewhat sexist, so we will change it a bit: "Clothes maketh the man/woman/person." It was cited by

Shakespeare and was written earlier in Greek. More modern takes on it are "dress for success" and "appearances count." Psychology calls it "impression management." You dress in a certain way to put forth an image that is intended to make a statement—or make a specific impression on others. It could be a statement about sports, being business oriented, being a professional, feeling casual, or whatever. However, no matter what you wear, your choice of clothing makes an impression. And that impression doesn't just have an effect on others, it affects you—and what you think and feel about yourself.

To make the relevance of this topic more obvious, we'd like to mention a couple of extreme examples. If you dress "dumpy" and comfortable, what impression might other people get? (Recall from the last chapter that one major drive we have is that we strive to make our life easier. If you went to a job interview dressed dumpy or casual, it puts out an impression.) Let's take this a bit further. You have undoubtedly seen people on the streets who you came to believe were homeless or had mental health issues. There is a good chance that the way they were dressed had something to do with your assessment. If you want to understand how this extreme example relates to "impression management," try a little experiment. Get the oldest, rattiest, and dirtiest clothes you can find. Put on a couple old coats, wear a worn-out hat, and add a pair of dirty pants. Walk around in public for a bit and see how you are treated by others. Also, pay close attention to how people look at you. If you have the gumption, go into a store that way. We will guess that this is something you won't do because you have a pretty good idea of how people will view you and how you will be treated.

On the other hand, you might try the opposite. Dress in a stylish business suit or nice dress and observe how others interact with you. You probably get the point here, but what we really want you to see is that how you dress and the impression you give others is a creation—one you determine through the choices you make. So let's try to bring this into a slightly different perspective. You can make your "impression management" choices based on conscious decisions, or you can allow yourself to just follow the unconscious habits you have established over the years. It is up to you.

You can instantly create a different you by changing how you dress and changing your appearance. Clothing is just one simple example of how we create ourselves, but there are many other things that apply. You can also create a new you by changing your attitudes and behaviors in your work life—immediately. If you complain a lot at work, deal with it in a direct and different way. How you speak, the words you use, the way you say things, and how you treat others all create impressions. They are all creations of who you are and how you are perceived by others. Just apply the two rules to any decisions you make by considering "doing no harm" and "doing the best you can with the resources available to you in the situation." It's all up to you. These are very simple examples, but the reality is that these principles can be applied to many other areas of life. You are constantly engaging in your own creation. It's wise to view your life that way, and it will provide you with a sense of control.

Boredom

Boredom has become a big problem today for many reasons. One reason is that we don't have to spend much of our time attaining security and safety. We have a lot of free time. The reasons that create boredom don't matter. What does matter is that if you experience boredom, it's most likely because you have created it. We say this because you have the ability to change it. You have the power to recreate what you do in life. Let's do a brief exercise to assist in making a simple explanation of this concept. We'd like for you to make two lists, which we will get back to momentarily. First, make a list of 10 places in your town, city, county, or region that you have never seen. Search some internet sources, if necessary. Next, make list of 10 things you have never done because you thought they were probably boring or were too much trouble to do.

If you took the time to make the lists, ask yourself the following questions. When is the last time you went to a free lecture? How about dancing or taking some type of lessons? What about going to a concert? Attending an exercise or tai-chi class? When did you take your last hike? When was the last time you took a class just for fun? Boredom is a creation that stems from our own choices. For example, we make choices to stay in and watch television or play games instead of getting out and doing things. The good news is that because we create our boredom, that means it can be changed instantly by us. If you look at your lists, you will see things to do and see that will not just relieve boredom, but also expand your creation. You have to make a conscious choice to engage in the activities on your lists.

Here are a couple of our examples. The authors live in the Memphis area and many children and teenagers consider this area boring. Of course, many teenagers say everywhere is boring. Several years ago two friends from England visited and one of them wanted to see Graceland, the home of Elvis. The other friend didn't care to visit it and didn't care much about Elvis. But on the tour of Graceland something unexpected happened—the one that didn't want to go actually cried and was overwhelmed. That is what can happen when you create an experience. Doing things you would not normally do is an act of creation. Memphis also has amazing historical sites that go back to early Spanish forts and the Civil War, the National Civil Rights Museum, Stax and Sun recording studios, and the 7th largest pyramid in the world. The pyramid, made from stainless steel, has a Bass Pro shop in it. Friends from Peru recently visited and were taken to a restaurant in the store, but before we went there, they said they'd seen Bass Pro stores before. But not this one. They left in awe at the swamp located inside the store, seeing the huge fish at their feet, viewing the interior hotel, riding its free-standing glass elevator, and lots more. The point here isn't about Memphis. The point is about everywhere. Every place has things you probably don't know about and would be at least amused when you saw them. When you find yourself trying to figure out what to do with your free time, take a look at the two lists you made earlier. Pick one or two things from these lists to do, rather than becoming bored. Remember, boredom is a choice. And within those words is a real hint about what causes boredom. It means that you have attained mastery over the lowest levels—you have safety and security, and you have achieved an easy life—at least in those moments of boredom. You have free time. Think about that.

Creating Your Future from The Present

If you feel stuck, trapped, bored, stressed, frustrated, or you are wallowing in any other negative feeling or emotion, creation is a way to get unstuck. The idea of creation—self-creation— allows us the freedom to change. *What you do in the now, the present moment, creates a different future that can evolve into even greater possibilities.* Of course, making conscious choices about self-creation is a process and it starts with a sort of self-excavation and self-evaluation. In this process, you evaluate a lot of things, but then, paradoxically, you cast some things off. To do it, you have to disengage yourself from some of your own truths, your beliefs, and disconnect yourself from the power that some of your memories exert over your decisions. In short, you have to de-identify from some of your identity. You have to let go of how you think about your mind, your body, your memories, your emotions and feelings, and your problems. You have to see that you have been living out a story and you have become stuck in it, like you are a character in a play or movie. In brief, you are playing a role. The ways in which you would describe yourself to someone else reflects the role you see yourself playing. The reality is that you have the ability to change your life story, or just walk out of it and create a new one. That's what creation is all about. Understanding this will give you true clarity, a personal epiphany. You have to take a close look at your story—the life you have created for yourself—in a disengaged, non-judgmental way. When you are able to move past your perceived limitations or barriers, you will begin to see your potential to create a new story.

The Neighbor's Problem

As the final part of this chapter, let's go back to where we started it. What was the best decision the neighbor could make about her social media websites spinning out of control and becoming divisive? That's an unfair question, because the best possible outcome is determined by her. But a couple questions helped her decide. In the discussion with her, the two rules from this chapter were first posed to her in terms of questions. First, she was asked if the situation was somehow doing harm? Secondly, she was asked if she was doing the best she could, using the resources available to her?

She believed that *some* harm was being done on her website but also that she had done the best she could, taking all the circumstances into account. Her efforts hadn't turned out precisely as she intended and she wanted it to somehow transform. But *she* wasn't doing harm. She was then asked, "What, exactly, was under her control in the situation?"

She had full control over the content of the website, meaning that she could delete posts and block certain individuals from posting things. But it was a time-consuming job that also created immediate dissension and anger from some resident participants. Even some residents who didn't like the negative comments wanted to allow them because of "freedom of speech." It was clearly up to her to decide if she wanted to keep trying to control something that appeared to produce some harmful side-effects or to start over and create something new. We all have choices. But it was apparent to her that *she* was doing no harm. Her decision was to let go of the control attempts and allow the situation to follow its own course. Over time, others who disliked the negativity and divisive comments made it known that the venue existed to make the community aware of issues. So some of the negativity continued for a while, and everyone had the freedom to respond as they wished. Gradually, nearly all the negativity just vanished from the site. Was that the "right" decision? Maybe there isn't a "right" decision in some situations, there is only a choice. But the key idea here is that the only thing you control—is you. You are either doing harm or you aren't. You are doing the best you can or you're not.

In truth, this is a situation all of us in the modern social media age face. We can join a social media app (application) or a vast array of website chat rooms—or not. We can post anonymously and post outrageous things that we'd never say to someone in person. This is a fairly common practice nowadays because almost every article posted online has a comments section. Whether or not such things are right, moral, or appropriate is up to each of us to decide. *Our advice is simple. First, do no harm. Secondly, do the best you can with the resources available to you. Don't lament what you can't get or don't control. Make choices to do what is under your control.* Finally, keep in mind that you are a creation, and a creation can transform in many different ways.

CHAPTER 4

Three More Truths About Life

We'll start with another true story from some years ago, but names and some details have been changed for the sake of confidentiality. This story is about a woman named Anna and some choices she faced about her marriage.

When Anna first entered the counseling office she looked worn out and unhappy. That observation was quickly confirmed. She was 26 years old and a mother of a 4-year-old daughter. Anna had been married for five years and she and her husband had gradually become more and more distant from each other. He was in graduate school studying business and was also working in a full-time job. She had a bachelor's degree and was working part-time in a medical office, a job she chose because of its hours and convenient location. She came to therapy because she "was unhappy and thinking about divorce." She quickly mentioned that their "sex life had dwindled down to nothing," and she said that her husband "had no ambition." She saw their future as bleak. She was also suffering from some depression and anxiety. Eventually she admitted she was sexually frustrated and was contemplating having affairs. She said what was stopping her was that she was too shy to do it and she was afraid of her parents' disappointment if she did act on her urges. She also had a strong sense of caring for her daughter and felt tied down by the responsibility of being a parent. What sort of advice would you give her? Would you ask her how she felt about these issues?

Anna had her basic needs met, like most of us do. She lived in a modest but nice apartment. Their bills were paid and she had the means to go to therapy. She had reliable transportation and they never had a lack of food or safety. As far as Maslow's levels were concerned, her essential basic needs were met. But she was struggling on the psychological needs level: the need for intimacy, love, friendship, and self-esteem.

One question posed to her was, "Could she achieve those higher needs in her current relationship and situation?"

She immediately answered, "No," as if she had already thought it through. She said that getting a divorce was the only way out. She then added that she was "trapped" and couldn't get out. So she couldn't go through with the divorce because of a great fear that engulfed her: *the fear of losing what one has.* In therapy we worked on strategies and methods to work with the resources and skills she had and "what was possible" given the situation. Whether or not the situation worked out was up to her and her husband, who saw no need for counseling. Life is about what you decide it's about. Deciding to stay where you are is still a decision, and it's one with consequences.

Entropy in Life

There is an important set of truths about the ongoing process of life. This next truth we will impart has been stated in a lot of places and in several different ways, and we have no idea who first expressed it. But the place where we'll quote it from is the 1999 movie *Entropy*.

Entropy is the tendency of any system or object to move toward a state of disorder. From the moment something is created or comes into existence, the process of entropy begins. Everything in the universe is subject to entropy including objects, social and business enterprises, living entities, and relationships. Unless a business is carefully monitored and needed adjustments are continuously made, the business will fall into disorder. In reality, the very act of organizing something like a business sets in motion its movement toward entropy. Relationships are no exception; they are subject to entropy, too. The same is true of physical objects: cars, appliances, houses, etc. Everything is slowly and relentlessly moving to a state of disorder and eventual failure, if not properly attended to or maintained. Paradoxically, entropy is a precursor to creation and progress. Because of entropy, some people seek out better ways of doing things.

Lessons are learned from failure. And the most important lesson of entropy is to pay attention and control the only thing you really can control—your choices and behavior.

The movie *Entropy* was about how a love relationship began, blossomed, and then collapsed leaving the individuals' lives in "disorder." It was made obvious that the people involved in the relationship had made choices leading to its demise. At the end of the movie, the main character (played by Stephen Dorff) was reflecting on his life and the collapse of his relationship with his true love.

He said, "The way I see it, there are three truths in life. You're born, you're going to die, and things change."

What is expressed in these three simple ideas are truths for every living person. There are certainly a lot of other things that are "true," and we'll get to some of those later. But for now, we will examine the ones mentioned above.

You Were Born. The first truth simply expresses the fact that you came into existence and it wasn't something you controlled. You can't remember being born or any of the time before it happened. You can't remember choosing to be born. You can't remember choosing your parents, choosing your genetic heritage, or choosing the life circumstances you entered. You didn't choose your facial characteristics, your skin color, your height, your hair, basic intelligence, or any innate athletic ability. Chances are that you'll agree with us that being born was something that wasn't under your control.

Maybe even more importantly, the truth is that *nothing that has ever happened to you in the past is under your control now.* The past is gone. Everything that has ever happened to you is in the past. Even the words you just read are now in the past. You can try to change how you think and feel about the past and attempt to control some of the consequences of your past, but what once was, is gone. Your past can be a bit like smoke. A lot of things in life are like smoke. Events sometimes just float away and dissipate into the fog of memory. But memories fade and our recollections change over time. People and relationships in life disappear. The past is gone. That is the truth about the linear timeline we exist within. Of course, the consequences of your past still exist, and how you choose to deal with them are up to you. But the fact is, you were born, and here you are.

You Are Going To Die. Secondly, there will be a time when you'll be gone—when your hand is pulled out of the water as an early chapter alluded. This is something we'll discuss again later, but how we'll explain it is simple and startling. *You are only here temporarily. Your time here is limited. Everything is temporary. Every relationship is temporary. Every job is temporary.* It is up to you to decide what you do with every moment in time before you depart this existence. *What you do with the time you are given reflects what the meaning of your life is to you.* It also reflects the purpose you might see to life. You either have a genuine, consciously chosen purpose in your life that guides your actions from moment to moment, or you don't. You can play video games, eat whatever foods you want, use drugs, argue and feel hurt, stay stuck in bad relationships, keep working at a bad job, stay in a miserable life, immerse yourself in pornography, or do whatever you want. You can choose to develop healthy habits or do nothing and let your health go wherever it goes. Or you can choose to do better things with your time and resources. It's all up to you. You can choose to be almost anything you want, as long as it is truly possible—and realistic. *But it's all temporary.* Your time here is limited, and many philosophies urge us to take advantage of every moment.

Things Change. Finally, there is the third truth: Things change. This truth is about entropy and creation. Chapter 2 began with a few descriptions of how people in the not-too-distant past had to manage life's necessities without any of our modern conveniences. Nearly everything about how we live our day-to-day lives has certainly changed since then. Back then people worked for much less money—if they could find a job near their home, because long commutes were more difficult to accommodate. Some people worked from sunup to sundown every day just to do what was necessary to survive from one day to the next. For most people there was no getting ahead. Their existence was a life focused solely on survival. They struggled to not lose what little they had acquired. Many people built their own homes and did whatever repairs were needed. It was a tough world, but a lot of people felt they lived in the best times ever. They engaged in simple pleasures and enjoyed what they could—or at least we hope they did.

They were probably right about living in the best times ever, based upon what they had known or experienced up until that point in time. As things progress, each generation has an easier and easier life as far as comfort goes. Electrical appliances, cell phones, reliable transportation, movies, television, computers, the internet, easily available food, safer housing, and countless other advances all make life a lot easier. Now, even people some consider to be poor have leisure time and have many things once thought of as luxuries. They can watch television, see movies, listen to music, and even use smart phones to talk, text, and search the internet. We know that there are still some people who struggle in their day-to-day existence, but few of them are reading these words. For the vast majority of us, we live lives of leisure that our ancestors of just a generation ago could not have even imagined. And the most successful of us have a lot of leisure time. We devote a great deal of our free time to sports, entertainment, games, and partying. Others spend time surfing the internet and engaging in whatever virtual pleasures they seek out. In reality, we choose what to do with each moment in time. But things change and there is nothing you can do to stop that from happening. You have to decide what the ongoing changes in the world we live in mean to you.

Easier Lives, Less Purpose?

Despite having an easier life, it hasn't necessarily led people to believe or feel that they have more purpose in life. In fact, for many people, this easy life has led to a malaise, cynicism, anger, depression, or a stoic attitude. Many people feel their work is a meaningless, daily repetition of a boring activity done for money and nothing else. Think of it this way. What is the most fun thing you do and the one thing you most look forward to doing? There's a good chance that it doesn't involve your work life. So most of us engage in a job or career that supports what we really "want to do." One consistent secret cited by self-improvement books is that it's smart to seek out work or a job that you enjoy. Warren Buffet said, "Look for the job you would take if you didn't need the money." But even many who manage to fulfill that goal can get completely enmeshed in a drive to do more and more. That occurs automatically unless you bring it into your conscious awareness on a routine basis. You have to make what you do with your time a conscious choice. People tend to live a life dominated by unconscious habits, performing the same actions over and over as if they were going through the motions that lead them toward an ill-defined end. Habits replace decision-making. Habits are useful to have and help create some order to life, but they still need to be developed consciously.

The concept of entropy is just as relevant to habits as it is to something mechanical that's on its way to breaking down. Habits can take the place of conscious decision-making and lead to a host of issues. For example, "mindless eating" is a habit. It is something that happens when our attention is drawn to something else. That "something else" can be watching sports, watching a movie, experiencing stress, or just feeling bad. Eating during those moments can become a habit that has consequences. Poor eating habits hasten the entropy—the demise—of your body.

In short, life becomes more disordered because we do way too many things without thinking about consequences that will eventually come. Relationships become disordered because we take people for granted or ignore important issues. Modern life can get hectic, chaotic, and lead to a sense of meaninglessness or hopelessness. Many seniors, young people, and those in between sometimes feel as if they are going through the motions of existing day-to-day. They feel as if they are simply existing, just drifting along looking ahead to some imagined better future. How many of us just want to make it to the end of the day so we can rest or sleep? Lots of people see their "better future" as just getting to bed at the end of the day. Today, there isn't the same sense of survival urgency that there was in the 1800s. In essence, our modern lives can lead to thoughts that everything is ultimately meaningless—other than just having as much fun as we can in the time we have. If having fun and relieving boredom is the main goal, it leads to people feeling trapped in an existence with no underlying meaning.

What matters is what we do in response to the change happening around us, and how much responsibility we take in controlling our own destiny. However, no matter what you do, things will continue to change. So, in brief summary, you are here; eventually you'll leave; and in between, things are going to change.

Creating Order in the Midst of Entropy

Another of all human beings' innate, built-in drives is to organize things so we can make sense of them and then try to control
them. We innately seek to create order, and it's designed to make
life easier. What that means is that our brains are wired in a way
that creates order—that is, the brain tries to make sense of the world
we live in. *Your fundamental beliefs are a way you have ordered the
world.* Whatever ways you live your life now are how you created
some order in your life. Habits create order in life. Relationships and
jobs create order. A place to live creates order, as do all of the objects
we accumulate. It's all about creating order to life. We form habits
to shape and control things, to create an orderly set of coping behaviors. Again, that's necessary and wise. The question is whether
or not your habits are a service to you or are an enslavement. Drug
use, alcohol use, overeating, and seeking to fulfill our sexual urges
can all be enslavements. Habits are ingrained, usually unconscious
behaviors that emerge at specific times, in specific places, and in specific circumstances. These times, places, and circumstances are cues
that stimulate habitual responses. That means they are an automatic
response to a cue from our environment. These habits can be beneficial, or they can be detrimental to our lives.

An example of a beneficial habit is brushing teeth. Most people brush their teeth before they go to bed. With nearly all of us, it
occurs at the same time of day and in a predictable sequence. The
thought that emerges ("Now I need to brush my teeth") at bedtime is
an automatic response to the time, the bedroom, pajamas, etc. It's an
ingrained habit you developed long ago. Negative habits can form in
the same way. Some people drink, use drugs, or engage in countless
other harmful habits when cued by a clock, a place, event, or certain
people. In a sense, all of our habits are attempts for us to create order
in the midst of entropy. They don't require thinking or decisions;
they are automatic responses to cues. The good news is that these
responses can be changed, if you want to change them.

Another way all of us have unconsciously created order is in
shaping our personality. *The way you see life, the things you believe,
and how you "instinctively" act in situations are all efforts to create*

order and are part of what you call your personality. In fact, the term "personality" came into use because psychology needed a way to organize its discoveries about why we humans do what we do. We do certain things habitually at specific times to create order, and we adjust so well to it that we seldom understand that it makes us act in automatic ways, reacting to life much like a robot would. Emotional outbursts, anger, jealousy, and other feelings are ways of coping with things that seemingly set us off. Those "things" are environmental "cues" that we can blame for our responses to them. We develop patterns of emotions, feelings, and behavior as ways of ordering our life. All of these things come together to create your personality. They combine to make you what you are. But are they the real you? Or do you strive to be something better, perhaps something better than you think you are right now?

The crux of this discussion on creating order is this: Our beliefs and habits form in ways that seem to help us make sense of the world, adjust to it, and manipulate it. What we usually fail to see is that our personality sets up the inevitable process of entropy. Disorder occurs as a natural process. Things happen and the world changes. Health issues crop up; important people in our lives move on; jobs change; and endless other changes and unexpected situations create disorder. Of course we try to adjust, but what happens is that we use our habitual methods to try to control things. And those things are often outside of our control. So our prior habits are often ineffective responses to new developments, but because they are so automatic, we blame the situation. We don't understand that we have to adapt to the new conditions. That's why many people fail to become something better and act in more noble ways.

In summary, your time in this world is limited, and your life during your limited time here is a creation you make. What have you created for yourself, and what *can* you create? *What do you want to create?* Let's end this chapter with a few more questions to consider. Do you believe you have a "true path" in life—some path that defines what and who you truly are? Are you on that path? Can you see yourself leading a life that has a sort of dignity and nobleness to it? Are you doing that now? What do you see as your meaning in life?

CHAPTER 5

Freedom and The True Path

We'll start this chapter with another real situation, but it also has names and specifics changed to ensure confidentiality. "I feel trapped," Evan said. "I have two jobs, one of which I hate, a wife, two kids, a house and car payment, and now I have to pay for the kids' school. It's too much."

"What is it you want?" he was asked.

He replied, "I want to be free; I just feel trapped by all that responsibility. But it's going to be years before all this ends. I'll do what I have to do, but someday it'll all work out, at least I hope so."

This is a story familiar to many of us. The vast majority of us have, at one time or another, felt trapped by our circumstances and responsibilities. We look to the future as a way to avoid an unpleasant present. How many high school students feel trapped? How many older children say they are constrained or controlled by their situation? How many people sit in an office or stay on duty at a job looking at a clock and just waiting for a particular time? All of us have felt these things in one way or another. But the situation above is a bit different. Feeling trapped can stem from responsibility. Evan felt trapped by the responsibility he had chosen and created for himself. When you accept and believe that you absolutely have to fulfill obligations and uphold your responsibilities, are you really trapped? If you believe that having a family is your "true path" in life, are the many ongoing responsibilities of having a family really a trap?

Evan made a long series of choices that led to everything in his life that he mentioned. He created his situation. He got married, had two children, bought a home and car, and decided (or at least agreed) that his children had to go to private schools. He worked in two jobs because of his family's financial needs, but he did mention that he liked one job. And more discussion with him showed that he liked being a father and was happy in his marriage. All of his concerns revolved around financial issues—money. Money and financial obligations are one of the most common sources of feelings of unhappiness or being trapped in life.

What Is Freedom?

Let's start with a few more questions. What is true freedom? Are we ever really free? Is anyone free? The answers to these questions are probably more complicated than we'd like. You probably have your own answers to these questions, but all we can do now is tell you ours. In some ways we are free; in other ways, not so much. This, of course, needs more explanation and is a good starting point to see what the idea of a "true path" is all about.

We'll begin by discussing the constraints of reality. You have probably heard others say something like, "You can be anything you want to be. You can do anything you really want to do." Obviously that's not really true. Lots of young men want to play in the NBA or be a sports star. It won't matter how hard they try or how much they practice, it's not going to happen for the majority people who have that dream. We all have a reality that is imposed on us by genetics. Here is a really absurd example that is relevant. Let's imagine that someone decides that he wants to get strong enough to jump to the moon. It won't matter how strong his legs get nor how powerful he becomes. No matter how hard he tries, it won't happen. That's reality. So while you aren't free enough to actually jump to the moon, you are free enough to try it. If you think about the second rule mentioned previously about decision-making (the rule that says *do the best you can with the resources available to you*), freedom becomes more understandable. It's all about the choices you have within the reality of your circumstances. For example, a person that loves basketball and wants to play in the NBA, but is not talented enough, does not have to give up basketball altogether. He can choose to accept that he will not play professionally and make a decision to play basketball in a recreational league.

Definitions of freedom all generally encompass the power to choose. It is the ability to act as one wants, given the legal and ethical constraints of a situation and the actual possibilities. Freedom is also the absence of subjection. It's about being independent in choice. We all have freedom in that we can choose our actions and decisions in any given moment. Problems emerge when we make choices that narrow our freedom or when we cede that power to someone else.

The truth is that we are all trapped the moment we enter the world. You are trapped by the body you were born with. You can do a lot of things to change your body, but a great deal of your physical potential is determined by heredity and genetics. For example, while some people assert they can change their sex, they remain "trapped" within the human species. More relevant here is that we are all trapped by time and the inevitability of age. Your body is programmed by heredity to change with age. Again, you can choose to do some things to alter the aging process a bit, but some things are inevitable. Live long enough and you'll understand that truth. You are also trapped by the society you live in with all of its perceived obligations and requirements. You are trapped by countless circumstances and conditions that surround you. You can move somewhere else, but no matter where you go, there are constraints. You can leave everything behind and start over, but no matter what, new circumstances and conditions will be there. You will have to adjust, and do so based on the limits the circumstances impose. And you will be there too. *No matter where you go, you will carry your belief system and habits along. Your beliefs are the prism through which you view the world and interpret things.* The things you believe are a big part of the trap. People who are chronically miserable and unhappy—and unsuccessful—are trapped in ways they seldom understand, and their underlying beliefs are usually the most difficult trap to escape.

The Prism of Beliefs

The following story is a simple example of how beliefs can trap a person and lead to temporary misery. One of us lives by a river harbor located in a large city. One summer the Army Corp of Engineers began dredging the harbor to allow cargo barges to make a safe passage up the harbor to reach storage silos that had been located in the same places for nearly two hundred years. The barges collected grain and cotton from area farmers and then shipped the products down river where it was processed. The dredging equipment ran for 24 hours a day pulling silt from the river's bottom to deepen the channel. The operation made a constant noise for about 12 days. Some neighbors who were aggravated by the noise of the dredging complained long and hard arguing that the police should stop the operation. This came as a consequence of their beliefs and the way they perceived the situation. They interpreted the situation as illegal and a personal affront to them. They called the local Mayor's office and other government agencies to no avail. For the first week of those 12 days they complained that the noise was "awful," "unbearable," "terrible," and used other extreme adjectives. (In truth, the noise was bearable because they got through it.) But most people didn't experience the noise as awful or terrible—it was just an inconvenience to them and could barely be heard indoors. It was a legal operation that was routinely scheduled and had to be done. The Corp of Engineers had a legal obligation, and the grain silos and the barges were using the river long before the neighborhood existed. And, of course, "entropy" happens.

River channels gradually degrade and fill in, meaning that the "order" created by the dredging eventually leads to disorder. That simply means that once you start dredging a channel, it'll eventually need to be dredged again if you intend to keep using it. Of course, that's a bit of information that most people never know and seldom care about. One interesting aspect of the dredging was that some parents used it as a teaching opportunity. They took their children down to the river to watch the process and explained history, how farmers move some commodities, why the depth of the river mattered, and how the government deals with it. Not many children have such a wide-ranging educational opportunity. Using a well-worn cliché, those parents made lemonade out of lemons. The real thing that one needs to see in this simple example, is how the extreme beliefs some people had about the situation were the cause of their discomfort. By labeling the dredging as awful, unbearable, not legal, and terrible, it set the person up to experience the feelings associated with those labels. The more they thought about it, the more they noticed it and the worse it seemed. The reality was that the noise was not pleasant, but it was the unavoidable situation at that specific time and place. The vast majority of the residents simply surmised, "It is annoying, but it'll end. Make the best of it." Now, something odd happened when the dredging ended after the 12 days. Almost no one realized that it had ended and it even took a couple days for people to notice. People had acclimated to the noise. Humans have a remarkable ability to adjust to changing situations. And that ability to adjust is built into us. We are programmed to adjust. If you have ever lived by a railroad or an airport, you understand what adjusting means. Our brain is wired to acclimate to such things.

Many annoying events are cues to our belief system. That means that some situations we are faced with provoke a sequence of beliefs and unpleasant feelings. Waiting in lines, sitting in traffic, and being around people you'd rather not spend time with are all examples. We are sure you could come up with your own long list of annoying things. The mental labels we place on these events and circumstances have consequences—internal consequences. When we "awfulize" such things, labeling them as terrible, horrible, and unbearable, it sets us up to have unpleasant feelings and be intolerant of them in terms of our behavioral responses. That is, we often have a tendency to label things quickly and we do so in extremes. In contrast, if we simply thought, "That's annoying," and then added, "This too shall pass," it makes the situation more bearable. The way you interpret an event can be a cue for you to respond to it differently. One way to look at this is that a lot of annoying or anxiety-inducing situations are opportunities. But the important thing to know is that once your initial belief emerges when a cue appears, you have to challenge the belief. Your first thought (belief) may be, "This is really bad." But you have to challenge it by making it less extreme.

While life does present us with some situations that are truly terrible, most daily events we label as terrible or bad are more like inconvenient and annoying situations. For example, someday you'll have a neighbor who has a new roof installed. You'll have to tolerate a few days of irregular noise. If you can't handle it, you can choose to go somewhere else until the noise ends. Or just make the best of it. If you get stuck in a traffic jam, be prepared to pass the time by having an audio book or engage in a mental activity that is soothing. Maybe at work you'll be tossed another assignment just at the moment you thought you were all caught up. The bottom line to this is that no matter what you do, life will throw things at you that you don't see coming. This is because things change and entropy is a reality at work all the time. You will find yourself in situations that appear to trap you. When such things happen, you still have freedom. You have the freedom to view it any way you choose. Your belief system will automatically interpret a situation, but where that instant interpretation leads can be the issue—good or not-so-good. You can control your beliefs by making them more reasonable and more realistic. Things that we immediately see as awful or terrible usually aren't that bad. Most of the time we only experience inconvenient events or annoyances, not terrible things. Some really bad things will probably come at you at some point, so it's wise to understand that most things we interpret as awful are not really awful. Making your extreme beliefs and interpretations less extreme is a way to give yourself some control over those situations.

Despite all the traps mentioned previously, you have the power to be free when you grasp what freedom really is. You have the power to find and embrace true freedom. This is done by examining yourself, challenging your beliefs about everything, making informed decisions, and then doing what's necessary to carry out your choices. Finding and living in genuine freedom isn't as difficult as it sounds, the question is whether or not you want to take that path. So, what does freedom *really* mean?

True Freedom

As previously mentioned there are many definitions of freedom. A dictionary definition is "the state of being free from the control and power of another." One-word definitions of freedom include "autonomy," "independence," and "liberty." How much autonomy do we really have? And can we ever escape the control and power of others?

Let's imagine for a moment that you suddenly get marooned on a beautiful deserted island. You aren't really "free" in the sense that you are trapped on that island. But aren't you then completely free of the "control and power of others"? Can't you do anything you want to do? Nope, and chances are you would figure that out right away.

First, there is only so much you can do on a deserted island. There are circumstances and conditions to contend with, and your survival will immediately become a paramount concern. You will immediately find yourself back on Maslow's lowest level of safety and security and those issues will become your priority. Your chances of survival, safety, and security would depend on what resources were available to you, combined with your knowledge and ability. (Remember the second rule? *Do the best you can with the resources available to you.*) What you'll do on that island is cope with the situation based on what you already know and believe, and you'll make use of the resources available there. The actions you would take would certainly be your choice, but they would come from what you had learned and come to believe after assessing the situation as well as you possibly could.

It is important to stress again that your first concerns would relate to Maslow's most basic level of needs—security and survival—food, water, and shelter. But again, let's ask a few other questions. Wouldn't your survival depend on what you learned from others in the past? Wouldn't your beliefs and knowledge about survival play a role in how you handled the situation? If you agree with that simple statement, you should be able to understand how our beliefs can either restrict or help us. Beliefs are the prism through which we view the world. They are how we interpret things. We'll pose another question here using the deserted island scenario. Would the way you decided to dress yourself there come from prior life influences? For example, if a suitcase of both men's and women's clothes washed ashore, which type of clothing would you think about wearing first? It wouldn't be a difficult decision would it? It would come automatically from your beliefs.

Would the shelter you decided to build come from things you learned in the past? The answers to all of these questions are pretty obvious and that's as it should be. Like all examples, the desert island scenario falls short of fully explaining what is meant here. The truth is that no matter where you are, there are specific circumstances and conditions you have to contend with. Your beliefs about things can limit your choices and restrict your freedom, so let's change the situation a bit.

Let's say you decided to visit Egypt. If you have ever done that, or visited just about any other Islamic-majority country, you know that Americans certainly stand out there. One obvious thing is that you probably dress differently than just about everyone else there. On a 12-day visit to Egypt some years ago, one of us witnessed American women touring the country being repeatedly harassed by local men. The women being harassed were dressed in typical American garb. This was an important issue directly addressed by the literature sent to the tour group well in advance of the visit to Egypt. Women were told to *not* wear shorts or short dresses and to avoid wearing tops that displayed much skin. Perhaps the harassment that those who ignored the dress warnings received wasn't "fair" or "right," but it was inevitable. The term "inevitable" relates to the reality of the situation. The tour leaders knew what would happen to Americans who ignored cultural warnings. They even reminded them about it when they arrived in Egypt. Nevertheless, several women insisted on wearing the same styles they wore in America.

The truth is, when we go to other cultures, we drag our culture's habits and our beliefs along with us. These habits, which are repeated behaviors we perform out of learning and our accepted beliefs, are automatic and largely unconscious. We don't think about them until situations are drastic and lead to consequences we don't expect or like. If you have ever had to dress in radically different clothes for some event, think about how strange you felt. That strange feeling came from stepping outside the beliefs you accepted about yourself. Those beliefs started forming in early life and then accumulated over time. Your beliefs are compiled into what you consider to be *your* truth. The real truth is that your beliefs sometimes represent a trap. The things you believe and accept as truth can keep you safe; they can explain things to you; and they can make life simple because you don't have to think too deeply. But beliefs keep you from being free. Beliefs are necessary, but they also constrain you. So here is a clue about beliefs. They represent you as an accumulation put together over time. To become a creation with genuine control, you have to cast some of your beliefs off and routinely challenge the rest.

Living on Automatic Pilot

Before we move on, a key point needs to be made again and stressed. Almost everything people do in modern society is automatic. We don't make as many conscious choices as you might think; instead, we automatically react to most situations. Our reactions come from beliefs that instantly emerge when various situations occur. That is, a lot of the things we do are unconsciously motivated and controlled. A simple example is seen when people say, "He made me mad." The reality is that it is *our interpretation* of events that "made us mad." How you interpret events is based on the things you believe. That's why we say that beliefs represent the prism through which we view the world. When we think we are making decisions, the range of choices has already been so limited by our beliefs, that no real choice seemingly exists. Think again about how you dress. You have restricted your choices. We'll say again that it's necessary to have beliefs—beliefs will form no matter what you do—but this sort of choice restriction occurs all the time without us realizing it. Most people never grasp this idea, but it's important to understand it if you want to gain the insight necessary to become truly free. It's almost like we operate on "autopilot" as we move from moment to moment. We will explain this in much more detail later, but here is a simple, common example that you can easily grasp. All you need to do is be around a group of people to witness it.

Watch people when there is an audible notification—a ding—from their smart phones. They will automatically look at it. If you think that they are making a conscious choice to look each time their phone "dings," you are probably wrong. It's not a conscious choice. It's an unconscious response that automatically occurs. It's like Pavlov's famous dog that salivated when a bell went off. It was a conditioned response that happened automatically. Pavlov was a Russian physiologist who put a dog into a restraint. Food powder was injected into a dog's mouth at the same moment a bell was rung. After a few times this was done, the dog salivated when the bell was rung. It no longer mattered whether or not there was food placed in the dog's mouth—when the bell rang, the dog salivated. Cell phones work the same way with most people. It dings; people look.

Try a little experiment with someone you know who is always linked to his/her phone. Challenge the person to turn over their phone and agree to not even look at it for 10 minutes as a "test." When it dings, or signals a notification, the person will automatically look toward his or her phone. Remind them not to look and when it dings, it'll happen again. They have become so unconsciously linked to their phone that their eyes will immediately look to the phone when it makes a sound. It is similar to what happened when Pavlov's dog salivated when the bell was rung. It's a huge problem on roads today as "distracted driving" dramatically increases. Of course, you already know this. That's why your phone is always turned off when you are driving, right?

The real point is that what we have called situational "cues" in several prior examples are the same thing as "dings" or notifications from a smart phone. The cues from our environment lead to automatic responses. Hit a traffic jam and a "ding" appears. It elicits pre-existing beliefs, automatic interpretations, and then produces an emotional response. Life is filled with such things. Your boss, parents, children, and the sight of a police car are some examples of such cues. Think about what you do and immediately think when you see a police car. That "special" person in your life who criticizes you is also a cue, a "ding," producing an automated response. Life is full of dings. Sometimes the automatic responses programmed in us are appropriate, but a lot of the time they restrict us and restrict our true freedom.

Back to How You Dress

Let's revisit an example we previously mentioned. When you get up in the morning and prepare to get dressed, what choices do you have? The answer for most of us is already in our closet and dresser drawers. Your range of choices are usually pretty narrow. The choices you made earlier in life created limits—your immediate choices of clothing are restricted by previous choices you made. You bought clothes you felt comfortable wearing, clothes that "fit" you in a style that you accepted as "you." However, the style you chose came from the influence of others. You might have been influenced by parents and grandparents who bought you certain types of clothing and praised you for looking so good in them. Even if you chose to do the opposite of what your parents wanted, they exerted an influence. You may have been influenced by friends or celebrities who you wanted to emulate or from those people whose approval you sought (peer pressure is a powerful force). You certainly have a few different styles of clothing for different occasions and activities, but the choices you have given yourself are limited by the beliefs you have about your-self and the society you live in. That isn't necessarily a bad thing; the point is that how you dress is deeply influenced by your beliefs about others and situations. And beliefs can be terribly restricting. Beliefs are perhaps the most restricting aspects in our lives, but they all started with things we didn't consciously choose.

Physical Attraction

It is rare in psychology classes to be told about why we tend to be attracted to certain types of people and less attracted to others. Why are some of us attracted to tall or short people? Why are some men attracted to slim women and others attracted to full-figured women? Why are some women attracted to athletic, muscular men and oth-ers to more average men or big-bodied men? Why are some men at-tracted to men and some women attracted to women? Why do some people like dark hair and others like blondes? We are often told that these preferences probably relate to the drive to find ideal reproduc-tion mates, but that isn't the real story. There is definitely a genetic in-fluence in such preferences, but many of these *preferences* also come from very early life experiences that are buried so deep in the uncon-scious you can't become completely aware of their basis. They relate to our earliest life experiences with body types, hair color, and other physical attributes that became associated with pleasant feelings. We form bonds early in life and these "bonds" are more like imprints that stamp themselves into our unconscious. Once imprinted, they automatically create preferences that will usually last throughout a lifetime. They are difficult to change and we aren't suggesting you try to change them. What we are saying is that it is a good thing to be aware that they exist. Being aware of them allows you some freedom of choice. It allows you to see the possibilities that exist.

Jobs and Careers

In a very real way, what we have come to believe about ourselves restricts us from potential jobs and potential careers. If you believe you are bad at math, you'll shy away from anything that requires the use of it. If you believe that you are shy, you'll avoid occupations that require a lot of interaction with others. People who have developed low self-esteem will often try to avoid being noticed. People who believe that getting the education needed for a certain career is too much work to do, won't even try. All of those apparent choices restrict possibilities. The important point is that they are very seldom *genuine* choices. Many apparent choices are based on deep-seated beliefs about ourselves that are buried deep in the unconscious. Unless you confront them and challenge them, they will continue to exert a powerful control and influence on you, and it's something few people ever realize.

We believe that there is a true path for everyone, a path that allows each one of us to become the best person we can be. It's a path that leads to true satisfaction and happiness. But our beliefs can obstruct our path. Money—and the perceived need for more of it—can greatly restrict our freedom. There is no doubt that money matters in the modern world, but how you choose to spend your limited time in this world also matters. Most people who have found a true path did so, at least in one way, in a career and a choice of jobs. It's not always an easy thing to find, but it's likely that you have some idea about what you'd really like to do to make a living. The sooner you realize what it is you truly want to do, the clearer your true path will become to you. It's accepted today that most people go through a series of careers, and often the ones we like most don't always start out paying the most. So we are encouraging those who are chronically unhappy with their work life to make a diligent search of themselves and their options. Options do exist, and there is probably a way for you to become what you most desire. In making such choices, it's smart to keep in mind the two rules: Do no harm; and Do the best you can with the resources available to you.

How Beliefs, Your Environment, and Culture Can Create Traps

There is no doubt that people come into this world on what can be called an uneven playing field. We've already mentioned that issues like looks, basic intelligence, and many other personal characteristics are greatly influenced by heredity. People do not start out on the same hereditary level. And the particular part of the world you enter at birth plays a great role. The environment you are born into, your family and friends you grow up with, the resources in your family, your neighborhood, and your culture impress and imprint beliefs and habits into you. It happens automatically in the same way our speech is determined by how the others we grow up with talk. But there are many other beliefs that get ingrained the same way. For example, it's very likely that no one is born a racist, and we can probably place the majority of the blame for racism on the factors in the prior sentences. In brief, people learn to be racist and the beliefs they adapt can get so deeply imprinted that they linger below the surface in the unconscious. They can also get ingrained into a culture that has actual physical boundaries—like a particular region, a city, or a neighborhood. Racism tends to generate more racism. In the same way, alcoholism and violence can run in families and particular locations. Whatever environment you are born and raised in will have a great influence on the things you come to believe. And as we have stated, the things you come to believe can create barriers and can trap you in them. Poverty is another barrier. There are several reasons that poverty tends to be an intergenerational problem in some neighborhoods and locations. In truth, people can be trapped by their environment unless they make *brave*, conscious decisions to change their situation. A complicating issue is that we can also get trapped in our cultural beliefs and expectations. We'd like to be able to help with all of those issues, but realistically, right now, it's just our words speaking to you—just one person. If you find yourself trapped in such a circumstance, you have at least three choices.

One choice is to complain about the situation and/or vaguely ask for help. That seldom changes things all that much and many people allow themselves to stay stuck, as if they are in a type of quicksand where they just sink deeper and deeper, making it harder and harder to escape. This first option really isn't a conscious choice and it relates to a tendency we'll discuss in detail soon. That is the tendency to take the path of least resistance. It comes from unconscious beliefs that tell you that you can't really change things and it's best to just stay there and endure your circumstances. It is related to the idea that you don't have control over your situation in life.

The second choice is to try to change the situation from within your immediate environment. This can be done within a family if the key family members really understand and accept their roles in the change. It is a difficult task and never really ends if you stay in the primary environment that you are fighting. Changing a community or the basics of a culture is a tough job and the relatively few people who do this find it a lifelong pursuit. It's the kind of thing Martin Luther King Jr. and Mahatma Gandhi did. Virtually all neighborhoods and cities have unsung heroes who do similar things in their locations. But it's a multigenerational task that often becomes a person's mission in life. It is a noble thing to do, but the majority of people simply aren't going to make the choice to do something of this magnitude.

The third choice is to make a new path for yourself. You have to transform your life and create a new life. It can mean leaving behind your culture and your neighborhood and starting over. But keep in mind that wherever you go, you'll drag along your beliefs and a lot of the cultural identity you have. These beliefs tend to stay in the unconscious—always exerting an influence—and they are very resistant to change. The difficulties encountered in making the second or third choice in such a dilemma explains why doing nothing—or taking the path of least resistance—is how most people respond. So nothing changes and it all gets passed along to the next generation. The second and third options require a diligent and very conscious choice, but they are the primary roads to change. In a way, it truly is the transformation of a person's entire life, and it is a brave act of self-creation.

If you think about the two rules (do no harm & do the best you can with the resources available to you), many people do harm to themselves and others by remaining in bad situations. This can be staying in an abusive relationship, keeping your kids in a crime and drug-infested area, or even continually socializing with abusive, angry, dangerous, or racist people. On the other hand, we know it takes resources to escape. Sometimes the only resource available is your own willpower. That can mean doing a lot of research and doing the best you can to obtain help. Useful information is available in libraries, at some social service agencies, colleges and universities, some churches, and within some governmental agencies. For those who don't face such issues, you might feel an urge to help others in such predicaments. You can. You only need to ask around to find out how. But you still have to make a conscious choice to do so and then follow through and do it.

Accepting Our Decisions and Their Consequences

The start of this chapter began with a very common, middle class dilemma—the true story of Evan. He was in his late 30s, well educated, and in a career. He liked one of his jobs and hated the "other" one, which was part-time. He took the other, part-time job because it paid well, was convenient, and it fit his schedule. However, it kept him away from his family too much. He loved his family and loved being a father. But his deep debt and the perceived need to send his children to private schools led him to see how his responsibility had gradually placed him in the position he now resented. He had made a long series of choices that led him to his current situation. Again, he came to feel as if he had boxed himself in, trapped himself, and that it would take more than 10 years for him to "see daylight." However, he embraced all of the decisions he had made, and regretted none of them. He also knew that there were consequences to the decisions. His beliefs about family responsibility, duty, and obligations were strong, and he willingly accepted the consequences. Since the extended time he spent at work was his most glaring issue, his work life became the focus of attention.

Evan came to see that the job he really liked—and also paid the least—was the key issue. He also liked the people he worked with at that job, but it didn't pay enough. He was asked by his counselor if he could find a similar position in his career where he could be paid enough so he could quit the part-time job. Of course he'd considered that before, but never seriously enough to take action. He was hesitant to ask his boss about it because he feared that they might think he was making demands and then try and find a replacement for him—the last thing he wanted to do was lose that job. It took some time, but eventually he searched around and found a job that might work out for him. It "appeared" to him after he spoke to various people. But then his boss approached him after he became aware of Evan's dilemma and his job search. After some frank and open discussion, Evan was offered a new, much higher paying job in the business he liked, and his boss had a great suggestion about sending his children to a private school. He took the new job, and it allowed him to quit his part-time job. Of course, that's not always the case in such situations. In retrospect, Evan realized that he had a set of beliefs that restricted what he had initially seen as his only options. His beliefs about his job prospects, his boss, and himself all combined to keep him from discussing the situation with his boss. Beliefs (the things we have accepted to be true about the world, ourselves, and others) can create traps and restrict our freedom.

CHAPTER 6

Living in a Skinner Box:
Superstitions and False Beliefs

Many years ago, one of us worked in psychology labs with rats. In one simple experimental technique, the rats were placed in what was then called a "Skinner Box," named after the famous behavioral psychologist, B. F. Skinner. Today the container is usually referred to as an "operant conditioning chamber." The box's sides and top were made from plexiglass, and it was about one cubic foot in size and had a small, metal bar protruding from a side. The rat could push the small bar downward. When the bar was pushed, a food pellet was dispensed into a small slot in the box. And, when the bar was pushed, it was accompanied by a "clicking" sound.

Typical "Skinner Box." From: Wikipedia Commons.

When we put a hungry rat in the box, the rat immediately started to explore the space. It stood on its hind legs exploring the box, and it moved from spot to spot, but eventually every rat touched the bar. When the bar was pushed, it made the "click" sound, and the food pellet was immediately dropped in the box next to the bar. The hungry rat quickly ate the food and started to re-explore, but more vigorously. Soon, the rat pressed the bar again as it moved around.

In this simple experiment, rats quickly learn to associate the bar and the clicking sound with food. Obviously, most rats eventually learned to press the bar over and over. That is, they learned that pressing the bar led to getting food, and the clicking sound became associated with the food. The food was a "reinforcer" for the behavior of bar-pressing. The underlying meaning of a "reinforcer" is that the food (the reinforcement) increases the behavior that apparently causes the food to appear. If you simply made the clicking sound when the rat was in the box, it immediately went to look for the food. That's the same way our smartphone's "ding" works on us.

A lot of what we know about reinforcements and the effect they have on behavior was first derived from the early experiments with rats in Skinner boxes. In fact, the way most people get paid in various jobs comes from our understanding of reinforcement and behavior. The way we dress, talk to others, and conduct business are also related to what these experiments uncovered. The field of economics has done a lot of research with people using variations of the method. But not by placing people in a Skinner box, of course.

Perhaps one of every ten rats in the box was observed to do something odd. The most extreme examples that took place were somewhat funny. What we'd see was the rat turning a circle in the box and then pressing the bar. After the rat ate the food, it turned another circle in the box and pressed the bar. And this was repeated again and again, sometimes with dizzying speed. What was happening was pretty simple and it related to the rat's learning.

Just before the first time the rat pressed the bar, it made a circular turn in the box as it explored. After consuming the food that was delivered, it made another circular turn in an attempt to repeat the behavior that led to the food. It pressed the bar again after making the turn and was again reinforced with food. Then the pattern repeated again and again. The rat had learned that if it made a complete circle in the box and pressed the bar, food was made available. If we can give the rat some human attributes, we would say it thought—or came to believe— that it *had* to turn in a circle before pressing the bar to get the reinforcement—the food. Of course, that wasn't true. All it had to do was press the bar. But it came to believe something different. In psychology, it's called "superstitious behavior." The important point being made in this example is that beliefs can develop the same way.

Superstitious Behavior

There are many, many examples of superstitions, like walking under a ladder and Friday the 13th. There have been people who got hurt after walking under a ladder and some bad events have happened on Friday the 13th. But then a lot of people walk under ladders with no problems and a lot of Friday the 13th days turn out fine. And bad things happen on other days and bad things happen to people who never walk under a ladder. Yet there are some "superstitions" that turn out to be true—or possibly true. For example, skeptics assert that prayer has no discernible effect whatsoever—that it's a superstition. In fact, you can search the internet and you'll be presented with what they call "proof" that prayer does nothing but perhaps briefly change the mental state of the person who prays. However, if you search various scientific studies published in reputable journals, there are a fair number of them that have shown prayer can have a beneficial effect. It's not our intention to sway anyone in this argument, but it does point out that some beliefs can get tricky... and changing people's ideas about the reality of beliefs is even more tricky. In the example of prayer, some people accept the findings showing that prayer can have a beneficial effect while others do not. Most beliefs have some validity, at least some of the time, and in some circumstances. There are a lot of sayings that people cite that demonstrate this. For example, you've probably heard the idiom, "Where there's smoke, there's fire." Is it true? Probably most of the time it is, but then there is chemical smoke, and some smoke is made without fire to intentionally conceal things. Then there is the saying, "If it looks like a duck, walks like a duck, and quacks like a duck, it's a duck." That's true, at least most of the time. Way back in 1739 a mechanical duck was made by a Frenchman, and since then a lot of artificial ducks have been made to closely resemble the fowl. They look like a duck; some of them walk like a duck; and some quack like a duck. But they aren't ducks, although some ducks have apparently thought so.

False Beliefs Versus True Truth

A belief is simply something you accept as a truth, but virtually all beliefs have exceptions. Our beliefs and habits form in ways that seem to best adjust to and manipulate the world we are in. Beliefs are the guidelines we use to organize our lives and determine our behavior. They are our mythology. To restate it in a way we did previously, beliefs are the prism through which we view the world. You cannot escape having beliefs. Our beliefs relate to our survival.

If you wanted to test the accuracy of your beliefs, you could start by making a list based on some of your strongest beliefs. For example, complete this sentence: "I believe that President Donald Trump...."

To test the accuracy of your beliefs about President Trump, compare what you write with 100 other people who completed that same sentence. It will not matter what you write. There will be some people who completely and totally disagree with you. Then try to convince the ones who wrote the opposite of what you wrote that you are right and they are wrong.

Now, here is the most relevant point in all of this. Very few people care what you think or believe—unless you agree with them. They likely only care about what they believe. And trying to sway someone's beliefs is usually a fruitless endeavor. More relevant here are our beliefs about ourselves, the people we have relationships with, and how we view the circumstances and situations that surround us. You could make a list of 10 important things you believe. For example, try to complete these sentences:

1. I believe that I am:
2. I believe that my biggest strength is:
3. I believe my biggest weakness is:
4. I believe my most important goal is:

5. I believe the most important person (or people) in my life is:
6. I believe my work or career would be better if:
7. I believe there are people in my life who:
8. I believe that my life would be better if:
9. I believe more people should:
10. I believe the most important thing in life is:

Of course there is a big difference between beliefs and facts. Beliefs have exceptions, but facts don't. Facts are truth, or *true truth* as some Native Americans term it. In simple math, one plus one is two. It is always two, without exception. A *true truth* is indisputable. Beliefs can and do change, but a *true truth* doesn't. Some sciences other than math get close to determining facts, so close that we all agree that their facts are indisputable. Things like the boiling point of water, the typical speed of sound, and distances are often cited as fact. One big problem, however, is that many of us confuse beliefs as facts. The truth about other people and situations is quite a bit slippery, and that's when we get into the realm of beliefs.

The term *true truth* isn't modern, but it has become more popular since the early 2000s. It is now being applied to self-help systems and coaching. In 2017, Meredith Atwood, the "Swim bike mom " issued a great modern definition of true truth as it relates to how we make excuses: "The True Truth—when you come to the place of honesty with yourself where you have stripped away all the excuses, lies and blame, revealing the changes and actions you must take to live the optimal life that you truly deserve."

Contradicting Your Beliefs and Extremes

A simple exercise all of us should do when we are being influenced by a strong belief is to challenge it. That is, find some exceptions to the belief. The easiest way to do it is to find something that contradicts the major belief. For example, let's imagine you wrote in number 1 above, "I believe that I am an honest and open person." Search your memories for a time when you were *not* honest and open. If you really think back through your life, you'll recall a time or two when you violated that belief. There is a saying that has been put forth in several ways, and one way is, "If a rule has any exception, the rule is wrong." So maybe the more appropriate way for a person to say they are honest is, "I believe that I'm fundamentally or usually an honest and open person." As to the other beliefs you might have listed, there is a simple way to challenge them. You can think of the exceptions, or even better, think about the things you do that show the belief is not exactly true. Maybe you wrote that you believe the most important person in your life is your spouse. Can you think of anything you did that might call that statement into question? Ask yourself, is that something you'd do or say to the most important person in your life?

One treatment approach in psychology and counseling is called "Rational Emotive Behavior Therapy" or REBT (Ellis, 1957). It asserts that situations and events are not the cause of the emotional reactions we have "because" of them. The "cause" of our emotional reactions is how we interpret the events based on the beliefs that emerge as a consequence of the event. It is our beliefs that stimulate the emotions that lead to our reactions. The bottom line to this idea is simple and profound: The root cause of many of our emotional outbursts, self-deprecating behaviors, and poor decisions are our own extreme beliefs. It is a set of "all-or-nothing" beliefs and "demands" of others that typically cause problems. Things like, "I must be perfect"; "I shouldn't be inconvenienced"; or "You should appreciate my efforts" are examples. Extreme beliefs typically include the words "should," "must," or "ought," or they are all-encompassing beliefs like, "All of those people are like that."

The founder of REBT, Albert Ellis, made a list of what he called "irrational beliefs." They are ideas that distort the truth of situations, are emotionally unhealthy, and are ultimately self-defeating. One of Ellis' key ideas is that the *belief* that a person needs to be loved and appreciated by all his or her significant relationships is irrational. Irrational beliefs lead to problems. Another irrational belief is that it's *not* okay to make mistakes. Other self-defeating beliefs are that it is awful or horrible when we don't get what we want, that unhappiness is caused by others or only by things completely out of our control, that worrying about danger is useful, that avoiding problems is a good way to deal with them, that your past controls your present, and that there is always a right or correct solution to every problem. Ellis and his many followers utilize these ideas, and many similar ones, in their therapy. Many of our most difficult issues in life relate to one or more of these irrational beliefs. One purpose of REBT is to expose these irrational beliefs and help people gain freedom from them so they can make better decisions.

Another way to look at irrational beliefs is that we often perform the same self-defeating behaviors again and again based on our faulty perceptions and interpretations. (It is the same thing as superstitious behavior.) For example, some people act like a dog chasing its tail. Why do some dogs chase their tail, running around in circles? The dog has a false belief. It believes it can somehow catch its tail and end the chase. It just needs to run faster! The dog fails to see the reality of the situation and is thus engaging in superstitious behavior. Repeated behavior based on a false belief is superstitious behavior. The same happens with us, sometimes in very subtle ways. There are relevant examples that have been frequently cited in certain types of relationship issues. One is that it has long been known that humans tend to be attracted to specific types of other people. Some people get involved in abusive relationships again and again. Why? It's like a dog chasing its tail, but with more serious consequences. The person thinks, "Maybe it won't happen this time." But that thought is based on false beliefs, not just about others, but beliefs about ourselves. Life is filled with false beliefs that lead to resentment and to the feelings that we are being treated unfairly. For example, many people believe that doing their job well will get them promoted. But doing your job well is more related to job security—keeping your job. In truth, research tells us that solving problems and showing the ability to do more is far more related to being promoted.

A lot of our negative habits, like chronic drinking or drug use, are human examples of the dog chasing its tail. With humans, we engage in drug use and drinking as a way to deal or cope with underlying issues. If you say, "drinking helps me relax and enjoy myself," you are saying that it helps you cope. Drugs or alcohol can give momentary relief. Eventually reality comes back and the need to soothe whatever the real issue is returns. Over time, the use of substances becomes habitual, and problems worsen because of what we do to soothe the problems that occur because of the negative coping behavior. The pattern is circular, and alcohol use is the classic example. Drinking too much or too often causes various problems that are directly created by the habitual consumption of alcohol. Using more alcohol relieves those problems temporarily but it worsens them over time. Another example of a negative "coping" habit is overspending. There are people who respond to crushing debt by going out and buying more stuff. Some people get out of a bad relationship and step right into another. The examples are endless. Try to think of something you have done time and again with the results being the same and undesired.

As we have already stated, you are a product of your past, a creation formed from combinations of a lot of heredity and early-life events. Then you have added on a lifetime of experiences. All of these things, plus countless decisions, have made you what you are. But you are a creation. Your past doesn't really control you. It does have an influence, but the degree of that influence is up to you. One method to demonstrate how our past doesn't control us is used with alcoholics in treatment. Some of them say they drink because they are alcoholics. The flip side is they are alcoholics because they drink. In some treatment approaches they are asked to move their arms up and down. Then they are handed a glass. They are then asked to place it on the table. They control their hands, and they are able to put down a glass when they decide to do it. Drinking alcohol requires that you lift a glass or bottle to your mouth. You control your hands and you can put it down if you choose to do so. Drinking chronically and too much can make you an alcoholic, but it's still controlled by the movement of your hands. In fact, it's a little discussed truism that there are a lot of former alcoholics around. Treatment centers don't like to acknowledge that the vast majority of *former* alcoholics quit on their own without treatment. How did they do it? They put the glass down and made a conscious choice to not pick it back up again. How we perceive and interpret things has a lot to do with our happiness. How much power you give to your automatic beliefs can be under your control. You have to make your underlying beliefs conscious, and become aware of your choices.

Why We Don't Change

One very real problem in making better choices stems from a basic human tendency. *We tend to avoid anything unpleasant and we often take the path of least resistance.* It's partly based on beliefs. Remember the earlier example of how some neighbors by the river that was being dredged stated that the noise was "horrible," "awful," and "should be stopped"? The more they focused on what they perceived as the unfairness of the situation, the worse they felt and the more severe their reactions became. The more they focused on the noise, the worse it got—at least as they perceived it. They came to believe that the actions being performed in the river were a personal affront to them that was undeserved and illegal. The underlying reality of the situation was that it was inevitable. The dredging happens about every 5-10 years. If you choose to live by a river harbor that has barge traffic, there will sometimes be noise. If the people living by the river didn't realize that fact, who is to blame? Really, the answer is no one at all. No one has any blame in this situation. No one can know all of the facts of all circumstances they are in. It's just the reality of the situation. Things change; entropy is real. So rather than thinking that it's horrible and unfair, why not just see it as an annoying, but temporary, event? And why not see it an educational opportunity? Such things happen all the time in real life. Countless people who were fired or laid off from jobs initially saw it as a disaster, but later said it was the best thing that ever happened to them. Some people decided to further their education. Some have said they were led to a job they had always wanted to do. And some people found their "true path" in life after something seemingly bad happened.

Examining the beliefs that restrict you and often control your emotions and feelings requires digging into them. You have to perform what archaeologists would call an excavation. You dig into yourself and find the key belief that is driving particular feelings and impulses. Then you examine the belief's accuracy, its exaggerations, and even its source if that's possible.

Recurring Problems

One way to really begin some self-excavation of your belief system is to ask yourself a simple question. It's this: *"What are the problems and issues that pop up in my life again and again?"* They might be lack of money, lack of education, being overcommitted, substance abuse, anger, depression, or repeated patterns playing out in relationships. Then lay out the beliefs you have about these situations and challenge them. There are endless beliefs we have about ourselves that can lead to recurring issues or problems in life. For example, if you have low self-esteem, you could start by listing the beliefs about yourself you think "cause" you to have low self-esteem. Maybe you are shy. If so, what are the beliefs you have about your shyness? Chances are that if you make a list of whatever issues have been dogging you, they will somehow relate to your beliefs. Once you identify the specific beliefs, you can evaluate their accuracy. They will often be an exaggeration. How can you know this? It's easy. Look at yourself realistically and find an exception to whatever belief you are examining. If you are shy or have low self-esteem, think of examples where you overcame shyness. If you see yourself as a failure, think of some things you have succeeded in or done well. Can you think of something you did that made you feel good about yourself? There are genuine messages in the exception to your rules—and beliefs can often function as rules for us.

We are stressing that you—and only you—should be in control of how you experience life. You have to have a sense of awareness and acceptance. You have to start seeing reality as it is and then accept the responsibility for how you try to control it and experience it. Let us say something clearly here that relates to the examples above. At a deep, often unconscious level, everyone fears rejection. There aren't many people who like being made fun of. To varying degrees, everyone harbors doubt about themselves. There are people who compensate for this by acting like extroverts, seemingly unafraid of being rejected. Then there are those who succumb to the fears and act shy by performing all the behaviors that demonstrate shyness. The simple secret here is that it's all an act. If you consistently act like you aren't shy, you aren't shy. If you act like you are shy, you will be.

The connection between your beliefs and feelings needs to be recognized in order for you to have the freedom of choice in situations.

Flushing the System

One part of the process of challenging your beliefs is accepting—or choosing to accept—what you have been given in life. This includes your looks, physical attributes, genetic influences, family background, and other basics like your intelligence. Then there is no one else to blame for any of it. It's just you. You can work on whatever shortcomings you might think you have, but it's important that you at least recognize them. A simple example is in physical attractiveness. You should dress as well as you can and present yourself as well as possible, but there are still basic realities. Looks do matter. It's demonstrated in psychology that people tend to believe that physically attractive people have a lot of other desirable qualities. And it's also known that physical attractiveness plays a big role in dating and relationships. It's not always the most important characteristic that influences others, but it is commonly the first thing noticed. It's also recognized that we tend to develop relationships with others who are in the same "ballpark" of attractiveness. The same can be said for intelligence. There is a reason why exceptionally intelligent people tend to have relationships with people who are also intelligent. The main point here is about understanding and acceptance. Such things are the way the world is. Fairness doesn't matter. All that matters is what is. Accept it and move on. Keep in mind, however, that many ways in which people present themselves to others is an act. That's normal. And acting in the ways you want to be can go a long way in becoming what you want to be. In addition, what matters most is what you control in your interactions with others and the world you live in. *You can only control what you do.* There are some things you simply can't control. It is a resistance to reality that causes our pain and struggle. Resisting reality can be thought of as trying to control things you don't and can't control. Part of accepting the reality of the world is in understanding that what you desire can't really be obtained through games of manipulation. You might occasionally get what you want that way, but in the long run, when you make it a game of manipulation, you lose what you most want... and playing such games changes you in undesirable ways.

In the 1970s some self-actualization gurus told us that life is a "game." There is no doubt that people play games with each other as they compete for the things they desire, but the typical idea of a game implies a loser. Maybe life is a game. But if it is, it is a game with long-term consequences to us the longer we engage in it. We'll return to the idea of life as a game in the final chapter.

CHAPTER

Assess Beliefs, Choose, and Do: The Magic of ABCD

There are a number of strategies designed to help a person make effective decisions in life. Some of these are very complex while others are simple. We think that keeping things simple is the best way. There are several reasons for this, but the most important reason is itself very simple. In the midst of a moment in time, when you are trying to decide on a course of action, there is seldom enough time to weigh everything that should be considered. As we have mentioned several times, most of us make decisions on the spur of the moment using instinct. Instinct is based on our unconscious preferences, past experience, and beliefs. But it's all unconscious, meaning that we are unaware of the issues affecting us. If you remember the ideas of "superstitious behavior," you should get this idea. Superstitious behavior is based on a false belief that is driving our responses. So here is a rather deep truth. Probably anything you identify as a "belief" has some truth and some untruth attached to it. Another simple example can demonstrate this idea.

We were taught that we needed to have a good education in order to be really successful in life. And the more education we have, the more success we can have. We have ourselves expressed this belief to many others and have essentially accepted it as true. So, is that belief true?

Yes. And also no.

In general, it's been true for us—and many others. Research reliably shows that the higher the level of education a person attains, the higher income he or she tends to have. There have, however, been many people who have been very successful without going to college.

On the other hand, we know a lot of individuals who got advanced degrees and, by their own admission, relate that their degrees played no real role in being successful—or unsuccessful. The first author taught in colleges for about 5 years and came to know some students who believed that obtaining a degree or a certification in counseling somehow guaranteed their success. The degree might have gotten their "foot in the door" for a job. In other words, the degree helped create the opportunity for an interview, but then it was totally up to that individual to meet the requirements of the position and succeed at the job once they were hired. Some of these individuals were saddled with huge debt when they left school and had only an illusion of competence to carry with them into the "real world." In summary, the belief about education being the road to success has a lot of truth in it, but it still has some flaws and exceptions. The outcome of education remains completely in the individual's hands. That's why it's simply a belief and not always a truth. It's not "true truth." Yet many of our decisions are made on the basis of a belief, and beliefs can lead us into traps.

What you'll find here is a simple process to help you get "unstuck" if you feel trapped in your life or in your daily routines. If you feel a sense of meaninglessness, hopelessness, or are feeling overwhelmed, we believe you can find your way out. You'll find a method to seek out your true self, find your true purpose, and develop the wisdom, strength, and courage to take advantage of what life has dealt you. You have a true path—a way to live life that gives you the freedom and opportunity to become the best you can be and experience happiness while doing so. What this chapter presents is a simple A, B, C, D process that you can apply to assessing situations, making decisions, and then taking a course of action.

Using ABCD

Albert Ellis' Rational Emotive Behavior Therapy (REBT) utilizes an ABCDE methodology to assist people in better decision-making. It's a good method but it requires a fair amount of time and discussion. It is generally used in treating *pathology*—severe life problems and various mental illnesses. What we present here is a much faster alternative that we similarly call ABCD that can be used in everyday situations.

ABCD stands for a simple, 4-step process used to evaluate situations and make informed decisions based on the information that is available to you. The process begins with quickly **A**ssessing the situation and challenging your **B**eliefs, followed by making a **C**hoice about what you can do, and then **D**oing what you have chosen. If your choice works out, that's great. If it doesn't, then you repeat the same process. The method stands in stark contrast to how most people move through life. Most of us tend to react to things automatically based on the beliefs that emerge in various situations. Before we present this method, there is a relevant piece of evidence we feel necessary to discuss about the decision-making process.

Automatic Decision-Making: Our Decisions are Made Before We Know They Are Made

A great deal of truth about human decision-making has been uncovered in recent biology and psychology research: that we are biological robots—reaction machines. Everything we do and feel comes from a complex interaction that is nearly automatic. Our perceptions are filtered through our beliefs and biochemical processes within the "wiring" of our brain. We can override our reactions through engaging certain brain areas, but it's a complicated process that depends on a lot of things like: our prior experiences, our beliefs, our habits, our genetics, and even the relative development of various brain areas. While many people pride themselves as being reasonable and rational, if they truly assessed all the things they do each day, they would find that the vast majority of things they do are just reactions to situations. These reactions restrict our choices and don't allow us to understand that what is truly driving our behavior are unconscious drives and underlying beliefs.

Before we get into the ABCD process, we need to make a strong but perhaps difficult-to-understand assertion about how the majority of our decisions are made automatically and unconsciously. We hope you can grasp the significance of this. Back in 2008, a follow-up study of earlier research results was published in the journal

Nature Neuroscience (Soon, et al., 2008). The study created a flurry of more follow-up research that essentially confirmed the results. The research evaluated decision-making. It did not evaluate the type of instantaneous reactions we might have to make while driving, but it looked at the types of decisions we make after a bit of consideration. The study employed MRI scans on the brains of people faced with decisions they had to make consciously after being presented with several choices.

What the study uncovered was that when faced with such decisions, the brain actually processes the situation automatically, and that *we are not aware* of what's going on. Before the moment that we "think" we have decided something, the decision has already been made unconsciously.

The brain scans showed areas of the brain that made the decisions, and the result was predictable and visible to the researchers looking at the MRI—*before* **the person faced with the choice knew he/she had decided.** That is, the person facing the decision was not aware that he or she had already made the decision, even though the researchers looking at the MRI brain scan could already see the decision. This seems contrary to everything we believe about ourselves, yet it's true.

Here is the bottom line to what this means. About 7 seconds before you make a conscious decision, the decision was probably already made by unconscious processes that took place in your brain. It's like the brain sends a signal to you with the decision, and you simply accept, without question, that you had somehow consciously come to a conclusion. Some people have cited this as evidence that we really don't have free will, that free will is an illusion. In some ways that's correct, because so much of what we do is done unconsciously and automatically. There is a sort of dark and murky area in the brain that makes a lot of decisions and then signals the decision to us so that we become aware of it—and we just accept it. Here is a really common example. Think for a moment about physical attraction you might have for another person. Typically, we know within a few moments whether or not we find someone attractive. It's automatic. In essence, a part of you—lurking below the surface—knows if you are attracted to that person before you are consciously aware of it. This finding has been confirmed by research time and time again.

But we aren't machines. We can override these seemingly automatic decisions. This is what the ABCD process addresses.

Assessing the Situation

To take a brief look at the process of ABCD, let's revisit the situation of Anna and her unhappiness (from Chapter 4). It is a complex dilemma and one that takes a fair amount of discussion. Later we'll look at how to deal with situations that require quick judgment, but for now we will stick to the ones that require a bit more consideration. Anna's situation is more global and chronic—and it is fairly common.

Assessing beliefs begins by clarifying the key parts of a situation and listing the beliefs you have about each of those parts. In Anna's situation, she starts by listing the people and main issues she mentioned during her sessions. As each person and issue comes out, the main beliefs about each of these are brought to mind. In Anna's case, her beliefs about her husband and the situation included his lack of ambition, her sexual frustration, a lack of intimacy, her daughter and her sense of responsibility to her, her job, and a sense of going nowhere in life—being stuck. Those are the main components of Anna's situation. Assessing beliefs related to a complex situation requires that these elements be organized in a way that makes sense to us. As we have already mentioned, humans have a strong tendency to organize things and attempt to make sense of them. So the beginning of organizing and assessing is to depict these issues in a manner that clearly shows the level of importance of each one—prioritizing.

In complicated situations like this, there is no better way to assess beliefs than writing things down. If one has the time, a really effective way to do this is to start by making a drawing that lays it all out. It's best to use a full page to do this and always draw with a pen or pencil, and not on a computer tablet. The reason why we recommend you do this is that drawing with your hand stimulates many areas of your brain. Drawing with your hand holding a pencil/pen engages more brain areas than doing it on a screen with your fingers. The more brain areas you use, the better you can access unconscious beliefs.

Below, we have provided a simple drawing that organizes Anna's key issues. Anna is at the center of her drawing, and all of the key issues are drawn as circles or "bubbles" that surround her. To summarize the process of assessment, the key elements of a given situation are first identified, then organized in a meaningful way, and finally depicted on paper.

When she first detailed her situation, Anna said she had already assessed her problem. Her initial vocalized decision was that her only way to deal with it was through divorce. She saw her situation as hopeless. What her counselor perceived immediately was that she had made that decision based on an instinctual "fight or flight" response. She had decided, at least on a conscious level, to run. But in the background, her unconscious had already decided that she couldn't do that. Instead, the eventual decision went to the third reaction in the "flight or fight" situation that a lot of people have never heard: it is "freeze." When Anna first entered counseling, it was clear that she had frozen, stopped dead in her tracks—even though she quickly related she wanted to get a divorce. The truth is, most people facing big decisions have done a preliminary assessment. A lot of our initial assessments are automatic and based on unconscious factors— the things we aren't consciously aware of. These quick assessments typically involve pleasure and pain, and searching for an easy way out—a path of least resistance. But what should happen is a person should take a good, honest look at his or her beliefs. As we have already alluded, part of the process is challenging each key belief. This should also be done on the same paper used for the assessment. So, next to each element made in the drawing, all of the important beliefs are listed. Here are Anna's primary beliefs as she wrote them on her drawing:

Challenging Beliefs

After each key belief is listed, each of them is challenged—which is the final step in assessing your beliefs. In simple terms, *it means coming up with a reason why each belief isn't precisely correct or accurate.* What you need to understand with this challenging process is that *we have a tendency to exaggerate when we cite our beliefs.* We tend to think about most things as "all or none," when in reality they are only partially true. For Anna, one of her beliefs was that her husband had no ambition. But he was in graduate school working on a master's degree! In brief, it is clear he had *some* ambition. He was also working full time. Anna's statement that he had "no ambition" was an exaggeration.

Anna also mentioned her sexual frustration. In her challenge of that belief, she was able to see that she was not *always* frustrated with her husband. Things started to change after they got married. She was frustrated *now*, but just realizing that their child entering their lives had changed things, made her realize that the issue was one they could work on. Also related to her sexual frustration was the lack of intimacy in their relationship. She immediately saw that it was associated with the sexual frustration and the arguments and "silent treatment" the two had engaged in. She had pulled away from intimacy in the same way that she perceived her husband had. This brought her to realize that her beliefs about her absolute responsibility to her child were affecting her relationship with her husband. That sense of responsibility wasn't wrong, but it did play a role in her pulling away from her husband. Finally, Anna's dissatisfaction with her job and the sense she was going nowhere in life was examined. The only thing she could challenge in that idea was that she *was* going somewhere in life, although it wasn't precisely where she wanted to go. It was clear to her that she had decided on that path, the path of being a mother to her child and that the job she took was the result of choosing the path of least resistance. She also mentioned the belief that her parents would be ashamed of her if she divorced and that she was afraid of losing what she had. She was able to see that her parent's disapproval might happen, but it would only be temporary. She also saw that a divorce would not cause her to lose "everything."

Disputing or challenging each of these beliefs helped clarify all of the various issues swirling in her head, issues that essentially caused her anguish and confusion. (Recall that in times of emotional situations, we tend to act automatically. Anna's automatic tendency was to avoid issues and take the easiest way out.) By using this simple process Anna came to see that everything in her situation had developed because of her own choices, and this realization helped her to further clarify things. Her assessment of her beliefs being challenged is on the following page.

I am going nowhere. ──> I am going
somewhere, slowly.

I feel trapped by my job. ──> I chose this
job. And I can choose to change it if
I'm bored.   (tied down)

I feel trapped by my responsibilities. ──>
  I wanted to get married, have a baby,
  and have this job because of its convenience.
  I like being a mom, having a husband,
  and working, some or most of the time.

He has a lack of ambition. ──> He does not; he
    is going to school and working full-time.

We have a lack of intimacy. ──> We both created
    it with our "silent treatments," we do laugh
    and have fun sometimes.

He can't fulfill my needs. ──> He has before, and
    he does when we feel close, though that's
    not a lot now. He could again if I let us
    work at it.

Choosing

After assessing the situation and challenging the main beliefs related to it, Anna's choices became obvious. When she was first seen
in counseling, Anna had already decided consciously that her only
option was to walk out of the relationship— to get a divorce. That,
to her, had appeared to be the easy way out. In fact, it became apparent that she entered counseling to somehow be encouraged to get a
divorce but something in her wouldn't let her do it. (Recall that we
all harbor a deep, unconscious part that exerts a powerful influence
on us.) However, getting a divorce had consequences she wasn't willing to accept. In looking at her beliefs and challenging them, she
was able to realize—and accept—that she had other options. It's not

necessary to go through all of them, but we'll relate what her choice eventually boiled down to, and it was a choice she made quickly after completing this part of the process.

One of the things she had realized, and openly admitted to, was the fact that she had argued with and complained frequently to her husband, followed by long periods of the "silent treatment." In a response similar to her own, he avoided contact and serious discussions with her. She was at least half of the problem, and she came to see that it was necessary for her to have several real and honest discussions with her husband. Based on all the possibilities, she arranged to have her parents keep her daughter while she and her husband went on a weekend trip where they could be alone and talk to each other without distractions. Her husband readily agreed. There, she planned to lay out everything she had been thinking, feeling, and believing. She had come to the conclusion that she wanted to try to save her marriage and that she hadn't been openly communicating with her husband. She even decided to show him her drawings.

She didn't see this choice as a last-ditch effort; she knew it was just a starting point. She knew that there would be more things that would have to be done. For example, she realized that she had been working in a job that was too easy and didn't challenge her, nor did it improve her abilities or allow her to use her true skills. It had been only a "temporary" solution she had chosen after her daughter was born because it was convenient. She knew she hadn't followed through with her earlier decision to further her career after her near-constant duties of caring for an infant began to subside a bit. She had chosen an easy route, but that decision made everything else fall into a pattern. She had created a "rut" in her life she had grown to resent. In her last session she said that she had taken a new job, one that she felt was challenging and fun, and that allowed her to utilize her skills.

There is one last thing we need to present in the choosing part of the ABCD process. It's been mentioned a couple times earlier, but we haven't placed it into this context. It is that when you are making choices, the "two rules" need to be considered. First, do no harm. Second, do the best you can with the resources available to you in the situation. Anna didn't want to harm her child, herself, or her husband. In addition, she decided to use all the resources she had to come to an informed decision about her situation.

Doing

The last step in the process is actually doing what you have chosen. You must follow through. Once you make a choice, you have to act on it. Make a plan of how you will do it and then make it happen. Hopefully, your decision works out. But, what if it doesn't? It's simple. Repeat the ABCD process. Assess the situation; challenge the Beliefs; make a Choice; and then Do what you have chosen. *Doing* is often the part where people slip up. The best choice is usually not the path of least resistance and doing it can be a bit uncomfortable at the start.

In the Heat of the Moment

Sometimes bad things happen fast. So fast that we tend to just react. So here's a simple example of how the ABCD process can work. Many of us have had times driving when another car cuts us off and seems to have deliberately created a near accident. Most people react rather quickly with an emotional outburst. In some cases, this reaction can be the beginning of a road-rage incident. When such an event happens, it is possible for you to train yourself to override your initial emotional reaction. You can start by instantly *assessing* the situation and becoming aware of the first beliefs that arise. The elements in the situation are you, any passengers you might have, the other driver, and the surroundings. Then come your *beliefs*. One of those is often, "That person did that deliberately." Maybe that is true; nevertheless, you could *challenge* that belief with the ideas: "Maybe they didn't see me"; "Maybe they are angry"; or "Maybe they were just being careless." Another challenge is simple. "So what?" Even if the other person did it deliberately, the challenge to the belief can be the same, "So what." It doesn't really matter; it's over and no one is hurt. Let it go and move on.

One other way to challenge the belief is by taking it to its extreme. Do you think the person driving the car that cut you off was driving around looking for you specifically and waiting to cut you off? Probably not. You just happened to be there at that moment in time. The really important thing to do in such heat-of-the-moment situations is to be aware of the belief that stimulates your feelings—

the moment that belief appears. You can train yourself to do this. The more you practice challenging the beliefs and reactions that seem to instantly emerge, the easier it will become to do so.

Another belief that often emerges in such instances is that you begin to search for a way to "get even." You might think, "I can't let them get away with it." But you can challenge that by simply thinking, "Yes, I can." The idea that you can somehow extract revenge or get even is simply immature, unwise, and self-defeating. More importantly, it can be self-destructive, which is an issue we'll talk about at length later. You can also challenge your beliefs by thinking back to times when you did something unwise or careless while driving. For example, most of the people who read this have used a cell phone while driving and found themselves drifting into the wrong lane. If you challenge the beliefs that emerge in any situation you face, your rational choices in the situation will soon become clear. The typical reactions people have in the car are to honk their horn, speed up and yell at the person, try to cut them off, or a host of other dangerous responses. But you have the ability to cut off the power to all of these beliefs by making a quick, rational assessment. This assessment is that *right now you are okay*. After this moment, doing something, reacting, or retaliating has the potential to cause harm to you or others. Many wrecks have occurred due to "road rage." Is acting on your emotions and irrational beliefs worth hurting yourself or your passengers? Is it worth going to jail for reckless driving, or worse? Remember, do no harm and do the best you can with the resources you have. The more you can practice doing this, the easier it gets. It can become an automatic habit that you create and control. Assessing your beliefs will help you gain control over the automatic emotions that emerge when you allow instinct to control you. You should also be aware that there are other rational choices in such situations. You can do focused breathing, pray a bit, or turn your attention to something else. *You get to choose* what you'll see as the most rational and effective course of action. Letting such things go and focusing on your own life is often the best choice. One question you can ask yourself in the moment is, "How will my choice in this situation make things better?"

Here is a simple example of ABCD in practice in a situation far too many of us have faced. These types of situations happen suddenly and can have severe and even tragic consequences if you do not have your feelings and reactions in check. One of the authors was driving to church with two young children one morning. The author was not paying close attention and apparently got too close to a man's truck that was in front of him. The man stopped his truck abruptly, got out and stomped back to the author's car. The author rolled down his window, immediately becoming angry that the man had stopped suddenly and approached, leaving too little space for them to drive around and leave the situation. The man began yelling and cursing loudly, coming close to the window and pointing his finger. Instantly, the author began to respond in kind with a loud voice. This only infuriated the man more, so the author began to quickly *Assess* the situation. The *Belief* the author had was that this man should not be allowed to block their car in and threaten them; however, no matter what the author believed, it was clear that this man was mentally unstable and ready to explode. The man did not know the author, so it could not have been personal; the author was just in the wrong place at the wrong time that day. Further, the author knew that if it continued to escalate, there could be a physical altercation or even worse if the man was carrying a gun. The consequences of those choices far outweighed the author's need to be right, especially considering the two frightened, innocent children watching from the backseat. The author *Chose* to de-escalate the situation. The author calmly told the man, in a normal tone of voice, that the family was just on the way to church and that no one was trying to cause any problems. The man continued to yell a bit, but the author did not respond—so the man eventually walked back to his truck and drove away. During the event the author *Assessed* and challenged the *Belief* about the other man's actions, *Chose* a different way of behaving to de-escalate the situation, and *Did* what he chose to do. It resulted in no harm being done to the man, the author, or the children. One really important thing to understand about this is that it all took place in just a few moments of time. If you have practiced this simple ABCD method, you can train yourself to do the assessment and belief challenging very quickly. It makes the options very clear to you and easily points out the most rational choices.

ABCD with Verbal Sniping

Let's take a moment and look at how ABCD can be used in less threatening, more common situations. A frequent experience all of us endure at times is what can be considered as verbal sniping that we receive from coworkers and sometimes even from those who love us the most. ABCD can be applied to such situations. The assessment involves the other person, our own feelings, and the others who are involved. If this is something you often experience, it is something you might want to start assessing on paper right now. Start by drawing a recent situation when someone said something to you that seemed to set you off or stimulate your emotions. List all the beliefs that were stimulated by the situation. Then challenge each belief. If you do this simple exercise, you'll see your possible choices emerge quickly. Depending on the outcome you desire, rational and good choices will become apparent. Sometimes the best response is to just smile, nod, and say "okay." But once you choose a response, follow through and do it. We aren't saying you shouldn't stand up for yourself—we are saying that you should consciously choose your responses to such things rather than let your unconscious react. Remember the question we asked previously and use it as a guiding principle when utilizing the ABCD method: *How will this choice make things better? Then think of the two rules.*

There Are Few Perfect Choices in Life and The Path of Least Resistance

One reality that is often expressed in varying ways is that life presents us with very few *perfect* choices. Sometimes people are mean and spiteful. Sometimes angry people deliberately try to create problems for others. Sometimes you choose to take a stand and fight back. But remember that very few situations in life provide us with perfect choices. If you think about politics much at all, you understand this idea. The same is true in relationships. When you think you have found the perfect "mate" for you, that's great. But if you wait long enough, you'll begin to notice flaws in that person and a few "imperfections."

Sometimes in life we are faced with situations where we have to choose the "lesser of two evils." When choosing potential jobs, people weigh things like salary, benefits, hours, and potential stress. Higher paying jobs may require more time at work, more responsibility, and higher levels of stress. While perfect jobs probably do exist, not many people are fortunate enough to find their perfect match. And even when they do, if you remember an earlier chapter, it's just temporary. Eventually the person will discover something about the job that changes how they feel about it. Everything is temporary. Things are constantly changing and evolving. Most situations require us to weigh all the pros and cons and somehow decide the probability of success in each of the various options we have. However, *most often we follow the path of least resistance.* What this can mean is that after making a choice, we fail to act on it because it can be difficult to make the change. We fall into semi-comfortable ruts and decide that following up on a decision with action requires more effort than we are willing to give. Oddly, this path of least resistance is not something that is totally conscious. It's another one of those murky things lying beneath the surface. And it can make the ruts we develop in life deeper and harder to alter.

A December 2017 research article detailed a clever study on "the path of least resistance" that was conducted by the University College of London (Hagura, Haggard, & Diedrichsen, 2017). The study demonstrated that when we are faced with decisions requiring us to do something, we are innately biased to take the path of least resistance. In essence, we are "wired" to do this unconsciously. We decide to do whatever takes the least amount of effort despite the fact that taking a different direction can lead to greater reward. Recall from an earlier chapter that one of our main drives is to have an easier life, and the path of least resistance fits that idea perfectly. (Remember too that a lot of the decision-making process is done even before we know that it's done!) Generally, people employ what are called "defense mechanisms" to rationalize their decisions even when their decision is clearly not what they consciously desire. That means we mentally diminish the higher reward behavior (i.e., minimize it) or utilize other defense mechanisms like denial. In brief, excuses are easy to make. There is an old saying that states, "Can't never could."

No matter what your excuse or reason is, if you constantly think of why you *can't* do something, you will never do it. You will never know if you can do something unless you try. And in order to try, you have to know that there is most likely a chance that you *can* do it. It might not be easy. Chances are it will involve some time, hard work, and determination. If it didn't, you would have already done it. Actions take some effort. Typically, the effort we put forth to accomplish a goal is reinforced by our life becoming a bit easier or more enjoyable by having done it.

Making Serious and Important Decisions: How Our Unconscious Contains Secrets

Back in 1997 the first author published a workbook entitled, *Staying Quit* (1997). The workbook is focused on the all-important drug abuse treatment issue of relapse prevention. The book remains in widespread use by treatment agencies today and employs Rational Emotive Behavior Therapy concepts and a variation of ABCD in its method. The idea behind the grammatically-challenged title, *Staying Quit*, is that quitting is easy to do. Millions of people have quit using drugs, alcohol, and tobacco. Most of them have quit lots of times! The real problem is that they can't *stay* quit.

Such is the nature of substance abuse—it is a habit prone to relapse. Any behavior related to obtaining pleasure or avoiding pain can reach a point where the behavior becomes a problem. Ceasing a pleasurable or pain-relieving habit is difficult. Drug abuse is just one such area involving pleasure and pain, but there are plenty of others. However, exploring the issues of drug abuse and treatment isn't the point of mentioning it here. What matters is how the unconscious parts of our mind exert a powerful influence on us.

You need to be aware of these unconscious influences. Remember that we have already mentioned how research shows that the unconscious makes choices before we know the choice has been made. Remember also that we have a powerful unconscious tendency to take the path of least resistance and that we are almost always seeking an easier life. Those three factors exert a powerful influence on us, and they are designed to keep us from changing. They are important enough for us to mention them again. 1) Your unconscious makes choices on its own and gives you the impression you are making decisions. 2) The tendency is to follow the path of least resistance. 3) You are seeking an easier and more pleasurable life.

You can't make these things go away, nor should you. The idea is to understand *when* they are influencing you so you can have the freedom to make conscious decisions.

The Unconscious Makes Secret Plans

One of the tasks in the workbook *Staying Quit* is for participants to make a list of their "risky situations." Risky situations include people, places, things, and situations that present the most likely opportunities for relapse. Relapse in this case is the act of using drugs or alcohol again after deciding to quit.

There are particular people who are linked to all individuals' drug use—friends who offer drugs and people we party with. Then there are places where drugs are available, and people who go there are encouraged to use drugs. That is, drug users tend to use with certain people, in certain places, at certain times, and when certain moods hit. There are emotions and moods that lead to drug use. Making a list of risky situations can produce interesting insights. In the *Staying Quit* workbook, clients are asked to make a list of the 10 most risky situations they face. Their lists sometimes include things like depression and anxiety, certain bars and events, and specific people.

Now here is the really important piece of information. More often than not, individuals who wind up in drug treatment programs will eventually relapse, and often they will do so many times before they really quit. But when they make the list of their "risky situations," they will invariably write down the *actual place* where they eventually relapse. They will write down the *actual situation* and the *actual person* who is involved with their eventual relapse. These details will be on their list of risky situations, but they'll never be at the top of the list. They will be buried toward the bottom of the list. This might strike you as odd, but it's true. And what it means is a bit "sobering," if you'll excuse the term. It means that they have a "secret plan to relapse." With most of them, it's usually so secret that even they don't know it. Sometimes it's barely conscious, but in treatment we try to bring it to their attention.

The relevance of this might not be quite clear to you. So, let's revisit Anna for a moment. What if we asked Anna to make a list of the people, places, or things that might happen to derail her choices of trying to make her marriage work and working on her career? Chances are that she'll write down rather precisely the things that she knows could make her effort fail. They will be written toward the bottom of her list. If you try making a list of risky situations related to the problem situations in your life, especially with problems that pop up again and again in your life, you'll probably be surprised.

Life is filled with choices and situations where we face possible failure or frustration. You can take any choice or situation you face and make a list of what might happen to make your choice *not* work. If your choice eventually fails to work out, you will likely find the reason on your list, buried somewhere toward the bottom. To be clear about the relevance of this discussion, what you need to see is that there are very powerful unconscious forces that are constantly in play when we make choices and decisions. We want you to be aware that you can bring them to the surface by challenging your beliefs and doing something we have yet to mention. That is, you need to get a handle on your intentions. *What is it you really intend to do? What is it you really want out of life?* The answers to those two questions are your real intentions, and they often lie below the surface of normal awareness, out of sight and out of mind. But they both directly link to your beliefs. You have the power to genuinely evaluate your beliefs and make what truly are considered to be free choices.

ABCD Summary

Let's provide a brief overview of the simple ABCD process. When you are faced with a situation or a problem, you start by *Assessing* the situation and the beliefs that are associated with it. For complicated decisions, we strongly recommended that you make drawings as we described earlier. Briefly identify the people involved, important events, and the situation. It's always a good idea to do it on paper. Next to each element involved in the situation (you, other people, events, etc.), write down the first *Beliefs* that come to mind about them. Then, challenge each belief by searching out a way to show that the belief isn't completely true. Keep in mind that many beliefs are exaggerations. The "exceptions" to each belief can be written just below the main belief. If more than one thing comes to mind, write it down too. If you use this process, what will happen is that your choices will quickly narrow down and become much clearer. This happens because you are bringing unconscious issues to your awareness. It generally doesn't take long for a clear *Choice* to emerge, especially if you consider the two rules (do no harm & do the best you can with the resources available to you). When you settle on a choice, *Do it*—follow through with the required actions you have chosen. Finally, if you come to see that your choice and follow-up actions don't lead to the outcome you expect, repeat the process using the new situation as the starting point. And if it fails to produce what you hope, consider going deeper by making the list of things that are likely to make your decision fail. There will be a secret buried there. That secret will reveal your true intentions, whatever they may be. Remember, sometimes our true intentions are just to take the easiest path.

CHAPTER

The Idea of a True Path

What is the story of your life? How have various events, count-less people, and endless choices led you to this exact point? As stated at the very start of this book, your story resulted from a combination of heredity, environment, and the many choices you have made up until the present moment. You can think about all those factors, but here is a reality about them. *They don't matter. You are here. You are always in the present moment of time, and what matters is what you decide in the present moment.* What matters the most is the direction you are heading *right now* and the path you are following *right now*. If you agree with this idea, then there are other important questions that emerge:

- Is this the path you want to be on?
- Is there really a right path for you to take?
- Are you destined to take a particular path in your life?

The idea of a "True Path" in life is very, very old, and it implies that each of us has a set of built-in potentials and abilities that are seeking to emerge and help guide our journey through life. Most concepts about the true path idea assert that we are here to fulfill some sort of deeper purpose. Maybe that's true. Maybe it's not. All we can do is cite our beliefs about it, but they don't matter to anyone but us. What is certainly true is that when we enter life, we have a lot of genetic predispositions bestowed upon us. These "genetic pre-dispositions" are potentials: innate abilities; some personality traits, and many physical characteristics. For example, basic intelligence is hereditary, but what you do with it is up to you. It's just a potential waiting to be developed or not. In a way, the true path idea is a bit like following your heart, but few people can really understand that idea. The reason is that for most people, their beliefs, emotions, and feelings get in the way of what we mean by the word *heart*. An example of this is, you might want to believe that it is your heart that is seeking to have sex with someone, but that desire probably isn't being motivated by your heart.

Happiness and The True Path

Early in life we start forming beliefs about the world and what we come to think will lead us to happiness. Money, power, fame, an important job or career, sex with particular people, and material possessions all are usually seen as a path to happiness at one time or another. Think back to your earliest love and how you craved to be with that person. You believed that if you could be with that person, you'd be happy. Think about things you wanted like new cars, a new house, a certain job, or anything else that seemed to be related to happiness at that moment. We aren't saying that these things don't matter; it's that they are seldom related to a true path and true happiness. They are all transient, temporary, and they fade in importance. Remember, everything is temporary.

The true path idea is more related to the genuine and real essence of yourself. It includes your innate drives and abilities. It implies that you have a genetic inheritance that was bestowed upon you that contains certain skills, virtues, characteristics, and abilities. It's something that urges you to become a bit bigger and greater than whatever you think about yourself at the moment. Though this isn't precisely the way we see it, it is as if you have a destiny preprogrammed into you. If that isn't clear to you, here's an example we think you'll readily understand. A vast amount of your physical characteristics like height, body build, coordination, and basic muscle composition are genetic. A boy born in America, who has the genetic makeup that will make him more than seven feet in height, have an athletic and muscular build, great coordination, and other natural physical abilities genetically bestowed on him, will likely be pushed into certain sports and be rewarded for doing so. In brief, it's as if he has a genetic destiny programmed into him. He can choose to accept it or not. To a greater or lesser extent, all of us have genetic predispositions that push us in certain directions.

One's "destiny" (or perhaps more accurately our genetic inheritance) can become distorted by a lot of things like visions of greatness, fame, money, influence, sexual urges, and power. But in a very real way, the true path reflects how we fit into the world. And it doesn't mean that we have just one "true" way that fits us, or just one path to follow. There are many roads that can lead to the same place. Therein rest the choices we face.

As we just mentioned, the idea of true path does not imply that there is only one right path for any person. In fact, the path changes for all of us as we move through life based on the decisions we make along the way. It is a progression that evolves and adjusts as we age, transition through different phases of life, and confront various needs and problems that emerge. *To us, the true path is more of a way of living than it is having a certain career.* Recall for a moment that we discussed *Maslow's Hierarchy of Needs* in earlier chapters. Our needs evolve and increase in complexity as we move through school, love relationships, career, parenting, and even later on. Let us emphasize what we just presented. There probably isn't one true path for any of us. There are continual opportunities and situations we find ourselves in, and we make choices, moment by moment. The choices we make can reflect our deeper selves—or not. Again, the true path is more like a way of living than engaging in a certain career or job. We think you will understand that pretty easily.

One way to evaluate your current true path relates to happiness and satisfaction. It is likely that if the things in your life and the things you do are creating a sense of happiness, fulfillment, and genuine satisfaction within you, then you are on your true path. Then too, the reverse is true. If you are unhappy and unsatisfied, you may not be on your true path. Perhaps the most relevant thing to keep in mind is that everything is temporary. Your past choices were temporary. Whatever choices you made in the past only led to more choice points as you moved down that path. Whatever you choose now will lead you to more choices. The more balanced you are, the easier making these choices becomes. The more aware you are and the more your beliefs are challenged, the easier it gets. Think back to some of your decisions earlier in life that have led you to where you are right now. Did you choose to stay in school and graduate, or did you drop out? If you graduated, did you go to college? For some people, these two questions can be useful in understanding the concept of how past decisions have created your present path in life. Now, think about jobs that you have had and whether your level of education played a role in your ability to get any of those jobs? These answers directly relate back to things discussed only a few moments ago. You came into this world with potentials. What have you done with them?

Alan Watts on Happiness

Alan Watts was a famous British philosopher and author who lectured to massive audiences about Eastern and Buddhist concepts. Watts was adept at making spiritual concepts relevant to Western life. A lot of his talks are found on YouTube. In one of his talks (Watts, A.), he addressed happiness and career. In a lecture he set up a scenario where an individual asks him for career guidance. He asked the person, "What sort of situation would you like?"

He then asks the person, "What would you like to do if money were no object? How would you really enjoy spending your life?"

Hopefully one answer that comes to your mind is the quote from Warren Buffet we previously mentioned: "When you go out in the world, look for the job you would take if you didn't need the money."

Watts advises that when you get down to what you really want to do in life, just forget the money. Why? Because, he says, "If getting the money is the important thing, you will spend your life completely wasting your time. You'll be doing things you don't like doing in order to go on living. That is, to go on doing things you don't like doing. It's stupid. Better to have a short life doing what you like doing, than to have a long life spent in a miserable way."

Watts adds that, if you do the things you really like doing, you can become a master at them over time. And eventually you'll find others who are interested in the same thing you do, which will create a demand, and you'll be able to make a living at it. He says that, "It's so important to ask this question: What do I desire?"

What We Desire

In the second chapter of this book, we presented what we called "the meaning of life." We defined it by saying that *the meaning of life is whatever you make it to be*. It's related to the question Watts said was important for each of us to ask ourselves: "What do *you* desire?" As we have already mentioned several times, we think most people desire to be something greater than they are now. People desire to make a difference. People desire to lead a noble and significant life. Do you agree?

Watts believed that based on our educational system's methods and western parenting styles, the confounding issue is that, "We want to control everything." At the root of the control desire is a hope to create technological omnipotence, a drive to create everything we can conceive of that makes our lives easier. He says this extends to a desire to make a completely predictable future. But that's not what the underlying human condition really wants, he says. "We want surprises in life." The drive to control things leads to disillusionment with the idea of power.

What Watts reveals in these simple statements are important points in finding your true path. And they are relevant to the dramatic changes occurring in society stemming from technological advances. We *are* seeking a sort of technological omnipotence, making our lives so easy that most people have nothing to do but just enjoy themselves. Okay, maybe it sounds great, but it'll become boring, at least that was Watts' take on it. Does reaching a sort of technological omnipotence mean people will have an easier time fulfilling the higher needs Maslow listed? Will having all of our time to enjoy ourselves lead to things like love, intimacy, self-esteem, self-respect and self-actualization? Perhaps it will; it probably depends on how we each respond to the emerging technology that already dominates life and promises to take over nearly everything. So, what we are left with here is Watts' big question: What do you really desire in life?

Striving for Superiority

Some of the ideas underlying the human potential and self-actualization movements of the 1970s derive their foundation from still another famous psychologist, Alfred Adler. Adler was the father of what is known as "Individual Psychology" and the founder of school counseling and career counseling. Most of Adler's work was done in the early 1900s, and some of his ideas have been in mainstream psychology ever since. Some of Adler's key concepts and terms are *inferiority complex, striving for superiority, lifestyle*, and being *goal-oriented* (Little, Robinson, & Burnette, 1998). For our purposes we'll just focus on a few of these key ideas that are relevant.

Adler related that we are often driven by unconscious forces aimed at the attainment of what he called "fictional goals." The earliest fictional goals we form in life are the result of irrational beliefs about ourselves, especially the idea that we are somehow inferior to (less than) others in one way or another. Early in life it is not just common—but normal—to conclude that others are bigger, more powerful, and somehow superior. Others around us control nearly everything. Thus, it's normal to somehow feel inferior early in life. That feeling of inferiority stimulates us to become superior. Adler called the drive to become superior "striving for superiority."

Nearly all of the goals we set are somehow related to us striving to become better than, more than, or superior to, what we are before the goal is completed. Whether it is a goal to go to college, get a better job, learn a new skill, or develop a new relationship, it almost always is an attempt to make ourselves better than we are—in one way or another. But don't make the mistake of thinking that our drive to become "superior" is always a good thing or based in something that's always beneficial or positive. An armed robber is striving for superiority. Robbing others might make him feel more powerful and have more money. A robbery can make the robber feel superior. So the drive of striving for superiority isn't always something positive.

Fictional Goals: Reasonable and Irrational

In a very real way, every goal starts out being somewhat fictional until it is fulfilled. The problem comes when an ultimate fictional goal is, in reality, unattainable or irrational. We don't want to make this complicated, so we'll stick to a very common goal many people have: financial security. That's a very reasonable, responsible, and rational goal in the modern world. But it can get twisted into something that can never be achieved.

For example, there are people who amassed huge fortunes and great power, but never attained their stated goal of *financial security*. No matter how much money these people attain, it's never "enough." Actually, in such cases, the goal wasn't really financial security. Such people often relate idioms like, "You can never have too much money." In that case, the goal can't be obtained until that person has *all* the money in existence. Maybe when the person reaches the point where there is no more money to be had, it ends. We aren't sure because so far no one person has achieved that feat. The irrational goal of amassing all the money that exists emerged from feelings of inferiority that transitioned to striving for superiority. But again, any goal you set is somewhat fictional until it's fulfilled, and goals are a very useful tool in creating a path in life.

There is a good chance that nearly everyone reading this book has a goal of achieving enough financial security for retirement. That's a both reasonable and wise goal to establish. There is a difference however between saying, "You can never have enough money" and saying, "I need enough for retirement." It may be true that relatively few people reach a point where they feel as if they have "enough," but if you think about Maslow's need levels, most people obtain enough to maintain the basic levels of security. Happiness tends to be more related to the higher-level needs. But some people, because of their circumstances and the beliefs that they have developed, seem to get trapped in the lowest of Maslow's needs—safety and security. This is a complicated issue that is vast in its implications.

An example of this can be seen in the gangster, drug-dealing lifestyle. It develops in lots of ways but usually happens in areas and cultures where poverty and crime are rampant and very observable to those who live there. In some cases, it emerges in places where the only visible "successes" and people who seemingly have power are gangsters and drug dealers. Remember that people strive for superiority, so in some cultures of poverty, getting rich and attaining power become the goals that emerge. Many of these people are in situations that foster beliefs that tell them the only way out is dealing drugs and violence. The point is that everyone strives for superiority. Everybody sets goals, whether they call them that or not. The important issue is whether or not they are rational and helpful in finding your true path. If your goals hurt other people, get you killed, or send you to prison, they are considered to be destructive.

Everyone Strives for Superiority

For the authors, our "striving for superiority" emerged in attaining more and more education. Going to college and graduating with certain degrees were our goals, but fulfilling the goal of graduation was driven by a desire to become something better, something more than when we started college. We knew that the accumulation of degrees would provide future opportunities. But we had to actually do something—take action—that supported the educational goal that would provide the increased future "opportunities." It's true that we never had to deal with the reality that people living in poverty and crime–ridden neighborhoods have to contend with. But the thing we want to stress is that attaining our degrees was all done in the quest of striving for superiority. We wanted to become something greater than we were. All we can say about the idea of striving for superiority is that the two major rules of decision making apply no matter what. First, do no harm. Second, do the best you can with the resources you have.

There is nothing inherently wrong with striving for superiority. In fact, it's a downright smart and wise thing to do, with a certain understanding. Everything you try to learn, try to accomplish and achieve, or just get better at doing can be seen as striving for superiority. So keep in mind that in life you are trying to become superior. In simple terms, "striving for superiority" is this: *You are seeking to become something better than what you are right now.*

The drive of striving for superiority influences everything in life—including relationships—and without being aware of it, we can become entangled in trying to achieve a goal that is ultimately destructive. Think back to the situation of Anna and her husband. Anna had a goal in mind concerning her relationship. She also had specific goals in mind for both herself and her husband. She was definitely striving for superiority in that what she wanted was a better life—for her life to become superior to what it was the day she walked in for counseling. Many of us sort of jockey for position in relationships, looking to take a position of power or superiority. We have a drive to control things, just like Alan Watts said. According to Adler, that's basically normal in the sense that it's what occurs most of the time. People naturally seek to control things. But the drive for control has consequences because others are driven by the same urges and impulses to control. In relationships, the attempts to control increase the pressure on both people who are involved.

To better understand this, visualize a pair of air-filled balloons that are in a confined space. As one balloon increases its pressure and size to control the space, it pushes on the other balloon. In turn, as the other balloon is being squeezed, it increases internal pressure and starts pushing back. But few relationships are conducted in a confined space. So it's pretty easy for one person to get squeezed out or just leave the increasingly pressurized situation. In human relationships, people get squeezed out of other people's lives all the time. So if you want to squeeze someone out of your life, let the other person know you want to control everything.

Then there are times when the pressure in a relationship becomes so great on one person that it's just too much for them to handle, and his or her bubble bursts. That could mean an emotional outburst, an emotional breakdown, or a total disengagement from a relationship. The real important thing to keep in mind regarding this is that trying to control things outside of your control will increase the pressure on you and anyone else involved in the situation.

Taking this discussion a bit deeper, let's differentiate between what Adler called irrational fictional goals and what we'll call beneficial goals. As we related, during our graduate school years, we clearly knew we were trying to become superior—to become something better than we were prior to graduate school. When you learn computer skills, you are striving for superiority. When you try to do anything better than you did it previously, you are striving for superiority. Those are beneficial goals. Right now, by virtue of reading this, you are striving for superiority. Even if you concluded everything we have written here is wrong, you are still striving for superiority. And whether or not you agree with what we have said, deep down you have come to the conclusion that you have become a bit more superior. Maybe you are more certain that your beliefs were right, or maybe you see a better way to make decisions. Either way, you have become superior to what you were before you got this far. If a goal has made you better at something, enhanced your life, produced some happiness and satisfaction, or improved relationships, then it has been a beneficial goal. What really matters here is that you have to decide whether your life is being driven by a goal that is unattainable or irrational and will lead to chronic unhappiness. Or, are the goals you have for yourself ones that are rational, challenge you, and are realistically possible?

Watts said to ask yourself what it is you really desire. What is it that you want in life? Ask yourself whether the path you are on can lead to where you want it to go or whether it is a road to unhappiness and sorrow. And realize that *everything* you do is related to your path.

Seeking Affairs and Better Jobs

We'll cite a few common situations to explain this concept a bit more. People have affairs. Statistics and polls tell us that over half of married people will have affairs. Affairs typically have some pleasurable moments or they wouldn't occur. Sex usually feels good. The fantasies that develop about the "other person" in the affair are often based on irrational fictional goals—certainly not always, but often. People who have affairs cite a lot of reasons for it, but what is less studied is why people *end* affairs. Affairs seldom last more than a couple of years, and most of them never reach that point. What is known is that the initial excitement peters out, to use a perhaps ill-advised phrase. But more importantly, it often becomes clear to either one or both people in an affair that the fantasy driving them—or the irrational fictional goal as we term it—is just that, a fantasy that reality can never achieve. And then there is usually guilt involved. Eventually, something forces a choice by one or both parties in the affair, and that choice ends it, often leaving some very hurt feelings and destruction in the wake. If you remember the example we used earlier about balloons increasing in pressure, you can think about the irrational fictional goal driving an affair as a balloon. At some point, the balloon bursts and the affair ends. But let's make something clear here. Affairs are about striving for superiority, something that always relates to goals. The striving for superiority is not about trying to have a better marriage or improved relationships. The person who has the affair does so because at some level the person believes that the affair will somehow make that person's life superior—better than it was. They feel that somehow the affair will make them happy or improve their life in some way.

An even more common example relates to jobs, or at least the quest to find a "better" job. During their career, many people are constantly on the lookout for a better job or career opportunity. The use of the term "better" should make it obvious that the search for a job and a career path is, in one way or another, all about striving for superiority. The underlying goals driving the search for a better job seek out more money, better hours, more prestige, and so on. There's nothing wrong with that, unless an irrational or destructive goal serves as the unconscious motivation. A sign that it's irrational is if the ultimate goal won't produce happiness and help you find your true path. In essence, all goals are aimed at somehow becoming superior, becoming and having something more than you started with. And your beliefs directly relate to these goals.

Sometimes we come to believe that fulfilling a certain goal will lead us to success. Attaining higher levels of education is certainly related to success, but it doesn't guarantee success, nor happiness. A specific example we can provide is of a young man who believed that obtaining a Ph.D. would make him happy. He believed it would bring him a lot of money and prestige. This man worked very hard to earn his Ph.D.; however, when he graduated it was difficult to find a job that would pay what he expected to earn. The intention underlying his goal of getting a Ph.D. (i.e., money, prestige, and happiness) did not take into account the fact that he had no real-world experience. Nor did he take into account the intense competition for Ph.D. jobs (due to the plethora of doctorate graduates) and that doctorate-level professors have to work many years before making much money.

He eventually took a job as a research assistant which accorded him little prestige nor recognition. But he did good work for a couple years. He gradually became resentful that his boss did not see his worth and promote him or at least give him a big raise. This resentment, based on his original irrational goal of money/prestige/happiness, built up over time and allowed him to justify doing less work at his job. He figured that he would start doing the amount of work that "he was being paid for," which was less than what he thought he should be making for "Ph.D.-level work." Eventually he had many problems at that job, lost a lot of people's respect, and was fired because his attitude (based on his irrational beliefs) had affected his work ethic. He then found himself on the path of an unemployed Ph.D. who did not have a job, was fired from his last job, and did not have any professional references to list for his next job application.

Using ABCD with Goals

It's easy to apply the ABCD method to any goal you may have, but it's really wise to use it on goals that might be unreasonable or irrational. We say that a bit ironically, because when a person has an irrational goal driving their behavior, they usually don't view it as irrational. So we suggest you assess the goals you have set for yourself and see where it goes.

Unless you are coping with a genuine psychological disorder (such as *anorexia nervosa*), it is not difficult to peer deep into yourself and get a glimpse of the unconscious beliefs driving you when you use this method. Anorexia is partly based on an irrational belief that "perfect thinness" is something that can be achieved. Adler cited anorexia as one of the most destructive fictional goals that existed. Explaining how the beliefs about perfect thinness are destructive and irrational is never sufficient when professionals try to treat people with anorexia. There are other psychological issues and personal problems that can't easily be addressed simply by challenging your beliefs about them, but it is often possible to discern how our unconscious beliefs exert such a powerful influence on our goals.

In a similar manner, the example of the person who desired a Ph.D. could be seen as being driven by irrational beliefs. How so? First, let's acknowledge that the goal of earning a Ph.D. wasn't irrational nor was it unreasonable because it was achievable. But if we rephrase and ask two questions Alan Watts put forth, the fictional goal and underlying beliefs can be seen. Watts would have asked, "What is your intention in obtaining a Ph.D.? What do you desire from it?" The intention of the goal and the underlying desire was money, prestige, and happiness. A Ph.D., in and of itself, isn't enough to achieve all of these things. So now, let's utilize the ABCD method on a very common goal.

Assess the Situation and Challenge Beliefs. Let's say that you want to find a better job for all the usual reasons. Again, it's a good idea to draw it out and write down some things on paper. You should start by listing the elements of the situation and the beliefs you have about each element. You could be in a dead-end job that has no opportunities for advancement or just decide you don't want to continue in that career. You are also aware of few opportunities elsewhere that you think might be good jobs to seek. That is your initial assessment of the situation. You could draw yourself in the center of a page at work thinking about a different job.

Next you should list the major and important beliefs you have about each part of your dilemma. It's a good idea to actually use the words "I believe" to start each one of these statements. Here are some relevant examples of a person's beliefs making her want to leave a job:

- I believe my job is boring.
- I believe I need more money.
- I believe that I need better work hours.
- I believe that I should develop more skills and utilize those I have.
- I believe I deserve more status and prestige.
- I believe that I'm better than my present job implies that I am.
- I believe I dislike my coworkers.

Next you challenge all the beliefs by coming up with something that shows the belief isn't entirely true or is an exaggeration. Here is what emerged in this job example.

- I believe my job is boring.
- Challenge: There are a couple of things at work I find interesting and that I enjoy doing.

- I believe I need more money.
- Challenge: I really just want more money. I've been barely scratching by, but I have been paying my bills nevertheless.

- I believe that I need better work hours.
- Challenge: Having better work hours will make my life easier. I just want better work hours. I would actually like to work fewer hours and get paid more. I've been working these hours for some time, so I don't really *need* to change; I just want to.

- I believe that I should develop more skills and utilize those I already have.
- Challenge: There are other ways to do this that do not involve getting a new job. I suppose I just want to get paid to do it. So far, I haven't been motivated to do this.

- I believe I deserve more status and prestige.
- Challenge: I want to be viewed by others as important and needed. I know deep down inside that I only deserve more status and prestige if I do something to deserve it. I can't say for sure what I mean by status and prestige anyway, except having people look up to me and think I'm smart.

- I believe that I'm better than my present job implies that I am.
- Challenge: I suppose I wish I was better and I hope I am. I guess it's something I need to prove and will need to put forth the effort to do so.

- I believe I dislike my coworkers.
- Challenge: I do like some of them. The ones I dislike, I dislike so much that it makes me have bad feelings for them. My actions have shown my feelings to them which has not helped the problem.

Choose. The next step is to make a choice. Remember that life seldom provides us with perfect choices. Also, keep in mind the two rules: Do no harm; and Do the best you can with the resources available to you.

In this situation, by the way it's been worded and the way the beliefs were listed and challenged, what becomes obvious is that the person has two genuine choices. The first is to stay in the present job and try to make things better. The second is to search out a new job. Hopefully what is also easily seen is that the person is striving for superiority, and keep in mind that striving for superiority stems from basic feelings of inferiority. There are a number of clues easily seen in what this person wrote when challenging her beliefs. Think about Alan Watts' questions: "What are your intentions; what do you desire?" Take a look at the challenge to each belief she listed to see the intention and desire. They are obvious. Here is the list of issues we see: boredom, money, an easier life, lack of motivation, desire to be important and to be needed, desire to become something better, and desire to get along with others and develop friendships. Overall there is a genuine sense of unhappiness and dissatisfaction. The most pervasive theme running through it all is that the individual lacks motivation to change.

Making a choice is made a bit easier by the challenging of beliefs. The paradoxical thing here is that by challenging each belief, both sides of the issue are simultaneously being weighed. You can't help but look at both sides of an issue if this method is followed. If the choice is to seek out a new job, what becomes apparent to this person is that the outcome is really in her control, assuming she has the motivation to do what is needed. The person can seek out a new job and only take one that pays more and has better hours. She has the power to decide if the new job fits what she is looking for, or if it is better than her current job. She does not have to leave her current job until her criteria are met. It's completely up to the person to learn new skills, put forth the required effort, and earn whatever status and prestige that comes with mastering the job. As far as friendships at work go, that too is up to the person. So, a choice must be made.

Do It. Once a choice has been made, you have to **DO** it. Follow through with actions that support your decision. Doing the thing(s) you choose to do is the most difficult step, and one that always takes some effort and courage. If this choice doesn't work out, repeat the process. Repeating the process will force the real obstacles and issues that are impeding you to emerge. As far as actually doing what's required to follow through with choices, keep in mind a couple factual pieces of information we have mentioned. We have a built-in unconscious tendency to take the path of least resistance. Doing nothing is often a lot easier than doing something. We also often have a secret plan to fail. That is, we set up situations in such a way to resist change. We set ourselves up to fail, to keep things as they are, and to follow the path of least resistance. It is important that we are able to recognize when reasons for not taking action are legitimate and when they are just because we are not willing to do the necessary work to follow through with our choice.

CHAPTER 9

Your True Path as a Mission in Life and The Dark Side

Countless spiritual concepts, self-actualization systems, human potential groups, and psychological theories urge people to develop a "mission in life." Typically, an idea of a mission in life first emerges when people are young and idealistic. Many youth want to change the world. That's often a good thing, but this early-life idealism will usually fade and be replaced by what might be called realism and practicality. Occasionally, after a person has achieved some success and developed a path in life, they will become interested in idealism and social causes once again. Depending on what the cause is and assuming it somehow betters the conditions for living things, it could be seen as a mission in life. So, in a genuine way, the idea of having a mission in life is related to one's True Path. However, the process of finding your life's mission—and your true path—is found while attaining Maslow's higher states. Recall that Maslow believed that after a person had met the basic needs involved with safety and security and the essential psychological needs (love, intimacy, & self-esteem), that self-actualization and even self-transcendence were the next stages of development.

A mission in life can be described in several ways. But it's always characterized by *passion*. Often what drives this mission is a cause that the person has great passion for—or sometimes against. We feel it necessary to next mention a prime characteristic that is found in a genuine mission in life as well as in the True Path idea. Both concepts *make the world a better place*. One's mission is always greater than the individual on the mission; it's a cause of sorts. *It is never self-serving and always helps other people or other living things.*

It can be for the betterment and good of your family, friends, school, community, church, animals, the surrounding greenspace, or the environment. Any cause that helps others or living things fits the concept. But it should be bigger than you. It will always be constructive and should never be destructive. It never deprives one group while giving to another. You should also feel passion for the mission. If you have a true passion for the mission, it will never feel like work. However, that doesn't mean it won't be difficult, or that it will be easy. We don't want to cite examples because those who understand the concept know what is required, and our intention isn't to steer people to our missions or causes. Developing a mission requires that you give of yourself, and you really never get back anything tangible other than satisfaction—and sometimes admiration or thanks from others. Many people who never go above the "psychological needs" level of Maslow's hierarchy have trouble just giving without receiving something in return. That's okay, and it's completely understandable. More problematic is when someone develops what he or she sees as a life's mission driven by what we'd like to refer to as "the dark side."

How Feelings Get in the Way—The Dark Side

Star Wars movies provide a great example of how feelings can get in the way of progress. Two of the plot devices that run deep in all of the *Star Wars* films are the "force" and "feelings." Those concepts have been driven into the deepest recesses of our unconscious by repeated media exposure to the Star Wars brand, something that is supported to a greater and greater extent by the digital age we are living in. The "force" is generally thought of as a sort of magical, mystical power or energy permeating everything in the universe. By reaching out with our "feelings," we can tap into the force and come to know truth and reality. At least that's how the early movies depicted it. The Star Wars "force" concept was adapted from Carlos Castaneda's writings as a way to permit and explain the conflict and superhuman feats of the *Jedi Knights* and the *Sith*, those former Jedi who chose to follow the "dark side" of the force. Several explanations of the force have been made in the films. The "force" has been described as an "energy field created by all living things" [composed of] "a microscopic life-form…that resides in all living cells" (*The Phantom Menace*, 1999). Perhaps that much detail is too much to handle for people who just like the movies. However, nearly everyone knows the term, *the dark side.*

Physics does, indeed, relate that the universe is saturated with an energy force concealed in all matter and perhaps everywhere. It is energy that exists in both dark (invisible) matter and in visible forms of matter. Then there are the forces of gravity, electromagnetic energy fields, and energy-containing plasmas. These things can all be viewed as a bit magical since it's not precisely clear how they *always* work, how they *always* exist, exactly how they connect, and what it might all mean. We can't say that by somehow tapping into these forces, one can know any truth beyond the laws of physics. Physics has discovered a great deal, but what *isn't* known about the universe far outweighs what *is* known. The relevance of all this to our topic might not be clear, so we will explain.

Starting in the 1950s, a strong movement began in psychology and counseling that is generally referred to as the "humanistic" approach (Rogers, 1951). It was an idea centered upon the assumption that people are inherently good and that the focus of counseling needed to be on the whole person rather than the parts. The human potential movement, the idea of self-actualization, person-centered counseling, and holistic theory all adapted concepts and techniques from the humanistic approach.

One of the fundamental and most basic techniques in "humanistic" or "person-centered" counseling methods is *understanding.* In psychology this type of understanding is often called *empathy.* Counselors often seek to help clients truly understand themselves by exploring, expressing, and clarifying feelings. Groups and individual sessions were frequented with the question, "How do you feel about that?" Then the feelings and responses were "reflected" back to the client in a restated way to clarify things to whatever extent possible. It was an effort to dig into feelings to get to the truth and the reality of situations.

The idea is that when feelings become really and truly understood, the inherently good part of the human will take over and do whatever is needed. Empathy is part of this process. Counselors are supposed to not only help clients understand their feelings, but the counselor also has to understand these feelings the same way the client does and then communicate that understanding to clients. Before we move on, we want to make it clear that we are not criticizing this approach. For a lot of issues and problems, it's a very effective method. For example, when working with teenagers, it can help them make good decisions about college, entering the work world, and deciding on an initial career. This approach can also help a person clarify their goals. But somewhere along the way, the idea began spreading into everything and eventually expanded into something it wasn't meant to be.

An example of this is that some schools began making students' feelings more important than their actual education and learning of the subjects. Giving students failing grades was discouraged because it might hurt their feelings. Soon, everyone had to get a trophy for "trying" because not getting a trophy might hurt their feelings. Our feelings about things gradually became far more important than reality and facts. In fact, feelings sometimes became more important than skill and knowledge. Feelings gradually became convenient excuses for everything. Feelings were used as justifications for all kinds of behavior. We aren't saying that feelings aren't important. We are saying that feelings can limit us by getting in the way. Feelings set limits and impede growth. Feelings can derail anyone from finding or staying on their true path. Feelings can easily become all that matter to a person. Feelings can make us the center of the universe, preventing us from seeing outside of ourselves, or really knowing what is inside ourselves. Our feelings can keep us from understanding and appreciating other people and can even cause us to push people away.

One truth about feelings can be understood by thinking back to all the times your feelings got hurt and how you responded. At those times you might have quit trying, lashed out at others, ended relationships, quit jobs, or any of countless other behaviors that ended something that was important. There is one more issue about the importance of feelings that calls into question our societal obsession with them. If our feelings are so important, why is it our belief that one person's feelings are more important than others? Why are my feelings more important than yours? It's simple. They are mine. Our feelings aren't always attached to reality, but they are attached to beliefs about ourselves that make each of us the most important entity that exists. That's human nature. In our minds, each of us is the center of the universe. There's nothing wrong with that as long as you understand it and don't allow it to control you.

In *Star Wars*, turning to the dark side occurred when a character's feelings got hurt by some perceived slight or not receiving the recognition that the character believed was due to him. The hurt feelings became consuming and the near-complete focus of the individual's conscious attention. Feelings were made all-important and they overwhelmed rationality and any concern for others. The dark side was outwardly expressed by behavior demonstrating that personal desires outweighed any possible higher mission. Power, greed, and control over others are manifestations of the dark side. Of course, all of that is from movies. Whether or not it seems relevant is up to you. We perceive truth in different places that can be used to explain such ideas to others. However, let's make this idea relevant to developing a mission in life and a true path. If your mission and path in life involves power, greed, or control over others, it doesn't fit what Maslow theorized about self-actualization and self-transcendence.

Feelings and Beliefs

The connection between beliefs and feelings is well established in psychology, and we have already mentioned it many times in this book. Until now, we have not gone into any depth about it. We'll state the conclusion we are going to reach about feelings before we try to explain how we reached this conclusion. *Feelings can be destructive, can be inherently limiting, and can be wrong* (Wanis, 2017). Chances are that you have heard the adage, "Feelings are not right or wrong; they just are." That's untrue. Feelings can be wrong. Not always, but sometimes. If you don't like the word "wrong," ask yourself if feelings can at least be *misguided or based on a false interpretation*?

To explain this, we'll utilize a couple of extreme examples. Let's start with racism. Racism is based on a set of beliefs. The beliefs associated with racism lump together people of a certain color, origin, or ethnic heritage. The beliefs are immediately applied to or projected onto individuals who fit whatever category or description the particular racist beliefs concern. Encapsulated inside those beliefs are strong feelings. All you have to do is challenge a person's racist beliefs, and you will observe feelings being expressed immediately. This can lead to emotional outbursts and destructive behavior. While the beliefs are the real issue, most people's behavioral responses are driven by their feelings about them. A person's behavioral response to what they feel can become highly destructive, as virtually everyone knows. That's why we have said that some feelings can be wrong. It just seems to be more accurate than saying that some feelings are misguided.

Political views are another extreme example, and one that has become more frequent in modern society. There are very, very few friendly and amicable discussions that take place between people who strongly *believe* in their political identity and who have widely different viewpoints. Keep in mind that one's identity is a very personal thing. Your identity is made up of all the things you believe about yourself and how you fit into the world. The feelings that emerge when parts of our identity are challenged can cause a person to become emotional and even angry. People driven by such feelings can become so enraged that at times they see it as their duty and obligation to do whatever is necessary to shut up or shut down the other side. Remember, this is all derived from underlying beliefs.

There are countless smaller and less severe examples of the destructive and limiting power that feelings can have. Sometimes just one word or a single snide comment can end a relationship. Even the way you look at another person can elicit feelings from them—based on what their beliefs tell them about the facial expression you have made toward them. These examples just mean that *it's easy to hurt some people's feelings.* There are plenty of families that have members who have sworn off ever seeing certain other family members because of perceived slights and insults—hurt feelings. This sort of situation also occurs frequently in the work environment. It is more difficult to deal with situations like this in a work environment because workers must come to work each day and face each other. Family members can just avoid coming to family gatherings.

Beliefs and Feelings: You Want to be Right

There is one more aspect about beliefs and feelings that we haven't mentioned, but it's important. We won't go into too much detail about it because it's a pretty simple concept. *People want to be right.* They will argue emphatically that they are right about their beliefs and that any opposing beliefs are wrong. This urge to be right blinds people. Ultimately, it boils down to the fact that people would rather be right than be happy. We insist that our feelings are justified because our beliefs are right. Our blindness stops us from considering the feelings of others.

There is such a thing as *"belief-induced blindness."* In a series of articles (2011), psychologist Daniel Kahneman called it "theory induced blindness." It is *"an adherence to a belief about how the world works that prevents you from seeing how the world really works."* It's related to the psychological process called *confirmation bias.* That is, when a person has a certain belief, he or she ignores and discounts whatever events are observed that show the belief is wrong. In brief, we tend to ignore exceptions to our beliefs. The events that confirm the belief are all that the person focuses on and sees. In short, when we only look at one thing, we often completely miss seeing everything else. Belief-induced blindness and confirmation bias are seldom conscious. In other words, when a person is influenced by those psychological processes, they are not aware of it. Think about this for a moment. When you have a belief about something and decide to look it up on the internet, do you stop searching if all results on the first page go against your belief? Do you immediately concede that your belief is wrong? Chances are, if your belief is strong enough, you continue searching until you find results that support your belief. This is a relatively common practice when people have strong feelings about something. They search and search until they find something that supports their belief in order to justify their feelings.

Rather than go further with this, let's ask what can, or should, be done to change the underlying faulty beliefs of other people—the irrational and false beliefs that drive their feelings and emotions? The answer will surprise you. *It's nothing.* We really can't do anything to get someone to change his or her beliefs. You can try to argue with people about their beliefs but it won't change much, except it may force the other person to believe even more strongly in them. But we aren't talking about other people. We are talking about you—and each of us—as individuals. Can you change *your* beliefs? Yes, sometimes. You can become better informed, more knowledgeable, and challenge your beliefs in the way we have demonstrated using the ABCD method. Look for exceptions to your beliefs. Rather than seeing these exceptions as exceptions, come to see them as truths that contradict your primary belief. Another thing you can do is simply accept that you don't always know the truth. You might find this surprising, but there is actually solace to accepting that you don't always know the real truth. Sometimes you just have to be okay with not knowing and keep in mind that any beliefs or feelings you have about some things create limitations for you. But there is another way to cope with feelings elicited from beliefs—maybe an even better and more effective way. And it directly relates to feelings. *You have to take the power away from your feelings.* You do that by consciously making your feelings irrelevant.

Making Feelings Irrelevant

With our strong societal urge to make feelings all-important, it may seem to be an impossible task to make your feelings irrelevant. So, is it possible to disregard your feelings? Can you ignore your own feelings? Is it possible to make your beliefs irrelevant? Is it possible to take power from them? Yes, it is.

In order to do this, it takes self-awareness and a lot of restraint—at least when you first start doing it. It also requires regular practice. Here is an example that comes to mind, and it's the first time that the first author of this book (Greg) can recall practicing this method. From 1985 until about 2010, Greg made literally hundreds of weeklong workshop presentations to counselors, psychologists, parole and probation officers, and others involved in treating offenders who were substance abusers. During that same time, he also taught numerous college and university classes for counselors, and he wrote and published several college textbooks. Countless times the same question was posed from someone in attendance at the workshops or classes. It was this: "What do you think about marijuana?"

One of the textbooks Greg wrote was entitled *Psychopharmacology* (Little, 1997). That book is about how drugs work in the brain and it includes a large chapter on marijuana. The research on marijuana's effects were reviewed in it, but the book doesn't issue an opinion on marijuana regarding whether it is good or bad or whether it should be legal. From the first time the question ("What do you think about marijuana?") was posed, to this day, the same basic answer has been given. That answer is, "It doesn't really matter what I think about it." Then the question is usually twisted back to the person who posed it: "Why does what I think about it matter to you?"

You might find the preceding paragraph unsettling in some ways. But it was a planned response done with forethought and with a specific intention. The reasoning began with the knowledge that countless experts and non-experts have already weighed in on marijuana. States hold votes on the legality of marijuana and in a vote, each registered "opinion" is equal. One more voiced opinion was seen as useless and would likely provoke too much discussion and possible arguments in the class. In all of the workshops and college classes that were taught, the focus was on the treatment of offenders and substance abusers. Opinions about what one person thinks about marijuana were irrelevant to the topic being taught and would be a distraction. Quite simply, we all want to be right and have other people agree that we are right. If others don't agree with us, then we want to show them they are wrong and we are right. *Being right can become far more important to people than being happy. Being right is a useless endeavor that involves arguing about beliefs.* It goes nowhere helpful and it is not beneficial to ourselves or others. With respect to the question of marijuana, the more you know about all of the research, the murkier it all gets. To make this personal, it's not that "I" don't have some beliefs about it, it's that I don't want my beliefs to sway or influence anyone else's beliefs about this issue. What's important to see here is that you need to recognize that a belief is just that—a belief. Beliefs don't necessarily reflect the absolute truth. In short, there was a conscious decision made to make personal beliefs and feelings about marijuana irrelevant. And the more that was practiced and was done, the easier it got.

Here is a more common example that many people can relate to. If you are married and intend to remain that way, it's wise to learn how to make some beliefs and feelings irrelevant. There are times in a marriage that your feelings don't matter, as other things can be far more important.

Certainly we aren't saying that you should make all of your beliefs and feelings irrelevant. You can't and you shouldn't. Some important beliefs and feelings should certainly be expressed. Understand though that there are always consequences when you verbalize or display these beliefs and feelings. Making a lot of your feelings irrelevant in day-to-day situations will make you a much happier person. Doing this can also make your true path a lot more apparent.

We'd like to cite another example of strong beliefs with strong feelings. Many people believe in God, the existence of the soul, an afterlife, or some type of religious or spiritual system. Then there are countless skeptics who deride these beliefs, deride those who believe in them, and attempt to impose their beliefs on the educational system and the media. Similarly, the believers on the other side often try to impose their beliefs. But it's all about belief, faith, and convictions—on both sides of the issue. There is no widely accepted scientific proof on either side, and the facts can be viewed in different ways. In short, it is *belief* that drives both sides. We aren't concerned with what you think or feel about this issue—*all that matters is what you do because of your beliefs.* From one rational perspective, here is what matters most. *If the belief gives solace and comfort and is not imposed on others—thus restricting their freedom—there is no harm. Harm is a result of the derision and intolerant behavior coming from the "other" side, whichever side that may be. People need freedom to choose.*

Chances are that there are many issues about which you have strong beliefs and strong feelings. The "smaller" ones are about other people and our relationships. Too many times insults, personal slights, and differences of opinion spin out of control when they are discussed. You can choose some example from your life that has caused hurt feelings and practice making your feelings irrelevant. You start by simply not saying what you think or feel. Sometimes you could simply say, "It doesn't really matter what I think…"

Of course, there are some issues that emerge into discussions that become deeply serious. When there are really strong feelings being shown on two widely different sides, what do you do? For example, if the topic of abortion comes up at a family function and you have gotten into heated arguments before with family members about this topic, it can be a good idea to try to *not* voice your beliefs and opinions about whatever is being said. Think of this as practicing making your feelings irrelevant in critical situations. You can say something like, "I'm going to sit this one out," or "You know how I feel about abortion; let's just talk about something we can agree on." Or you can just walk away and talk to someone else. The only thing you "lose" by doing this is the potential argument and hurt feelings that could occur. Remember what we said earlier—certain beliefs are deep-seated, and by and large, they do not change due to a discussion with someone of opposing beliefs. Over time, it gets easier to censor yourself in this way and not say everything you are thinking or feeling, especially if you are consistent. What you'll likely find is that your relationships work better and you will *feel* better. You'll feel more emotionally secure. More importantly, you'll be happier and more satisfied.

On the other hand, there are times and places when expressing your feelings and opinions is the right thing to do. There are times when you should fight for the things you truly believe in. So vote, join petition drives, lobby for an important cause, and help agencies with the issues that are dear to you. But ask yourself how important it is to create an angry argument at a family function over a cause or belief. Sometimes all that's needed is a simple comment to end such things: "You already know how I feel; there is no purpose in discussing it any further."

Being a Victim vs. Being a Survivor

Bad things happen to people; unfortunately, they happen to everyone. If something bad hasn't happened to you yet, just wait. It'll eventually find you. Some people are victimized by others or circumstances so badly that they are left with deep scars: physically, mentally, and emotionally. The effects are long-lasting and profound. All of this can lead to extended periods of depression, anxiety, fearfulness, anger, and more. If any of that describes you, we urge you to seek out professional help. Many people who were victimized turn their victimization into their mission in life. They become advocates. They start or assist in shelters designed to serve different types of victims. But, in order to reach that point, they have to first come to see themselves as "survivors."

There are some obvious reasons why many people embrace a victim's identity. A lot of people addicted to drugs and many people who have committed crimes often relate they are victims. Being a "victim" bestows an identity and a set of built-in excuses. It can be a sort of "club" with some ill-defined membership status. What it does is make the past responsible for the present. It makes other people responsible for the present. It can make society responsible. It can garner sympathy and be a way to absolve the self of all responsibility. It can be an endless game that shutters the person from finding happiness and their true self. Identifying as a victim will keep you stuck and will keep you from having the freedom to choose a new identity.

Many people who have been victimized try endlessly to overcome their victim's identity. But "trying" sets up excuses for failure. As *Yoda*, the wise Jedi in Star Wars stated, "Do, or do not; there is no try." It can be a hard pill to swallow, but it's a necessary one. So what this means is simple. Keep exerting an effort until you succeed. Sometimes you really have to just move on, get on with life and leave the past behind. You have to come to see yourself as a survivor. And that's not a trick. If you were victimized in the past and are reading this now, you are a survivor. Remember that one of the main ideas we have stressed again and again in this book is that the past is gone. You control what you do right now, in the present moment. If your main identity is "victim," you are choosing that identity. The reality is that you are a survivor. You have survived the past circumstance(s) that victimized you.

One idea that is seldom expressed in psychology about the victim's identity is related to the unconscious influencing our beliefs and the deep-seated issues we have. This is a really deep and important idea, which is about to be expressed in different words. In fact, it is so deep, it needs its own book. But we are just going to spell it out here. You can take it for what it's worth or you can leave it.

You can't really change the unconscious stuff. It'll be there as long as you live. But you can become aware of it and understand its influence, at least temporarily; just know that understanding it doesn't just make it vanish. It never goes away. Usually it sinks back down out of awareness. So, what do you do? *You have to make it irrelevant.* The escape from a victim identity starts with accepting that you are a survivor. Change what you believe by challenging the beliefs that make you feel like you are a victim. And eventually, you have to make your feelings about being victimized irrelevant. It's definitely not easy and it will take continual practice to make it happen.

Practice

We'll end this chapter with a few more suggestions about how to practice making feelings irrelevant. First, you have to become aware of circumstances and situations where one or more of your beliefs are being stimulated or challenged. And you have to become aware of your feelings the very moment they emerge. *You have to make a conscious decision to be self-aware, and you must exert some self-control.* You have to have a pre-made decision to hold your feelings and opinions in check. Now, we'll give you an example.

Let's say that someone brings up politics during a discussion. And, as usual, beliefs are expressed, an argument begins, and then heated feelings come out. What do you do when someone asks, "What do you think?" One good answer is, "Hey, I'm just listening." Then just observe and listen. As it continues, you will probably come to see that whatever you believe about that topic won't really matter unless you agree with one side or the other. Of course the opposing side will want to argue with you. Remember that people want to be right about their beliefs and feel justified in their feelings. So resist sharing some of your beliefs and feelings as practice.

Here's another hypothetical situation. Imagine someone tries to take advantage of you by asking you to do something for them or to give them something. You immediately feel some resentment and a bit of anger. Don't express either feeling. You can choose to do what is asked or just say rather matter-of-factly, "I can't do that." Then let it go. You might feel the urge to snap back at the person or take revenge, but here's a little secret. People try to "take advantage" of others all the time. It's something humans do. There is no use in getting angry because of a trait that nearly all humans have. Just decide if what they ask is something you really want to do or not. What do you say if the other person asks, "Why can't you do it?" Have a prepared answer. One answer we really like is, "I have too many other responsibilities and have to be sure I can fulfill them." You are not obligated to give any further information, but if you are asked about specifics, you can just say there are way too many of them to discuss. Then move on.

Here's a real-life situation about making feelings irrelevant. A friend (we will call her Tess) had a neighbor who was not very friendly. An erosion problem developed on their shared property line and Tess couldn't get the neighbor to respond to her requests to jointly solve the erosion problem. Tess repeatedly tried calling and texting the neighbor to make suggestions about what they could do to solve it. The neighbor would sometimes answer and would agree that it was a problem that needed to be solved, but she never followed through by getting back to Tess on whatever had been discussed. The neighbor would also sometimes accuse Tess of causing the erosion problem, which was not true. The accusations caused Tess to have angry feelings and increased resentment toward the neighbor. Tess finally decided to take care of it and pay for it herself, but no contractor would complete work on the property line without the neighbor's permission. Many other steps were taken in an attempt to solve the problem over the course of a few years—while Tess's and the neighbor's soil was washing away. Finally, Tess found a company willing to fix the problem for a large amount of money. Tess knew that if she waited for the neighbor to help pay or respond to the problem, she would just harbor ill will and the erosion would continue to get worse and devalue her property. So Tess sent her neighbor a written message stating that she was going to have it fixed and pay for all of it. During a subsequent phone call, there was some questioning and one last accusation made that Tess caused the problem. Tess immediately wanted to respond in anger, but she restrained herself and allowed her feelings to become irrelevant—so that the big problem could be fixed. By doing this, the tension was eased and her neighbor's attitude changed completely. At the end of the phone call, the neighbor agreed to let the workers on her property and the issue was ultimately resolved. Tess realized that the only way to completely resolve the problem and move on was to make her feelings about her neighbor irrelevant and focus on finding a solution she could live with.

CHAPTER 10

Character and Freedom2Change

Nick Saban is currently the head coach for The University of Alabama's football team. He's one of the most successful and well-known coaches in history. However, his record as a coach isn't our focus; it's what he stresses to his student-athletes that matters. It doesn't matter if you are skeptical of college sports—just read what he says.

Saban routinely delivers a speech to his incoming team each year. Most of the new team members are 18 years old and just out of high school. In his talk to them he emphasizes the idea of developing and having *character*. In one of his recorded talks to his team (2013) about character, he stated, "It's an accumulation of your thoughts, your habits, and your priorities: What you think, what you do, and what's important to you." He stated that those parts (thoughts, habits, & priorities) "determine the choices you make, and the choices you make, make you who you are." Discipline is the key, and he says discipline is a choice. His simple definition of character is: *"The right thing, the right way, the right time, all the time."* Do that and you have discipline and character.

The right thing for each of us is determined by our true path. The right way is usually a bit more obvious. We are pretty sure that most people have a sense of right and wrong. Some people, however, don't care about doing things the right way. But the truth is that one's true path and happiness depend upon doing what's right and following a set of principles in life. Think about a job or task that you rushed through and didn't do properly, just to be done with it. Chances are you or someone else had to redo part or all of the task. You made a decision that cost you more time and effort than if you would have done it right the first time. The "right thing" usually betters our life in some way and allows us to keep moving along our path.

Unconscious Barriers

There are many barriers people confront in doing the right thing, in the right way, at the right time, all the time. People take shortcuts and get lazy. Remember that one of our primary drives is to have an easier and easier life. We take the path of least resistance and do so without making real conscious choices. In our modern world, it's not that difficult to have an easy life the majority of the time. Having a victim's identity also creates a barrier. But the biggest barriers come from all of those beliefs swirling below the surface with feelings attached to them. Taking shortcuts, being lazy, being a victim, blaming others, and wanting an easy life all get in the way of happiness. And they are barriers to you finding your mission in life, your purpose, your true path, and what we call your true self. As to finding your true self and your mission in life, we assert that there are certain personality characteristics and traits that are necessary prerequisites.

Freedom2Change

Encapsulated in the term "Freedom 2 Change" is a list of fundamental principles and guidelines that lead to character and happiness. They are: Freedom; Responsibility; Education; Enlightenment; Diligence & Decency; Obligations, Observation, & Optimism; Motivation; Two (2) Selves; Commitment; Honesty; Authenticity; Nobleness; Genuineness; and Epiphany. Each of these is briefly discussed.

Freedom

The entirety of this book has been about gaining freedom and taking responsibility for it. In essence, it's about gaining freedom from the self-limiting beliefs and feelings that we harbor. It's freedom from your own unconscious forces. As we stated in the prior chapter, you can't just make these things go away. The unconscious stuff will always be there. You can understand your beliefs and feelings and even challenge them, but ultimately you have to make them irrelevant. And this takes practice. One easy way to practice is to make real and visible changes in yourself. Establish healthy habits. Dress for success. Change your attitudes. All of us have freedom, probably much more than we suspect. You can change a little, or you can change just about everything about yourself. You can literally create a new you, with some effort. Change how you act; change your habits; change your attitudes and demeanor; or simply change how you dress. You have freedom—accept it and take responsibility for it.

Responsibility

Personal responsibility for our lives rests on each of us whether we like it or not. You control your actions. You determine what your hands do, where you go, what you do, and how you respond to things. You determine whether or not you do drugs, drink, or engage in questionable activities. You determine your level of honesty, friendliness, and all of your other personal characteristics. Your health is highly dependent on your behavior and your habits. You are accountable for your actions, and everything you do has consequences. Accepting personal responsibility takes awareness and making a conscious choice. If you do this, you can find happiness and success along the way.

Education

Throughout life things change, though you might not be aware of how much. Even what we think of as knowledge has an expiration date. In *The Half-Life of Facts* (2012) Samuel Arbesman related that there is a good portion of all of our knowledge that will soon be, or already is, obsolete. It's astonishing to think that knowledge changes, but people change and the world we live in changes. Current knowledge appears to have an expiration date. One of Arbesman's examples is that doctors used to assert that smoking was good for us—a "truth" that was accepted for years before the discovery that it was, in fact, very, very wrong. About half of medical knowledge is obsolete every 8 years or so. We were once told that ulcers were *caused* by stress, but now we know ulcers are *worsened* by stress and are usually *caused* by infection or long-term use of nonsteroidal anti-inflammatory drugs (NSAIDS). Depending on what you read, drinking red wine is good for us, or according to the most recent research, even a little alcohol is bad. And that will, no doubt, change. There are countless more examples, but you get the point. Think of how the ways we live life have changed dramatically over the past century. Knowledge changes and evolves. Technology is adapting and evolving so quickly that a lot of what we see as factual knowledge is obsolete, just like how to use a buggy whip became obsolete knowledge. In the beginning of the book, we mentioned houses that were being made by what is essentially a massive 3-D printer using a type of recycled concrete-like material. There are also houses, barns, offices, and buildings that are unloaded from a truck in a singular, big, rectangular box. A button is pushed, and the structure automatically unfolds and constructs itself. All you have to do is connect it to water and electricity. It is move-in ready. Some of these structures even have their own built-in water and power sources. When you want to move it somewhere else, push a button and it folds itself back up into a box. Things like this will be seen as not so special, or as commonplace, in the future. There is so much more we could mention here but it's unnecessary. The way to think about this is that you have to always be a student of life. You have to always be learning and adjusting to new things. You have to continue your education. But keep in mind that most of what you probably think of as fact is based on beliefs. Some of it is obsolete and/or inaccurate. No one completely and totally understands this world, but some people are better at it than others. The better you are at understanding, the more effective you will be and the happier you *can* be. Contrary to belief, ignorance is not bliss. Ignorance is just that—ignorance. Bliss comes from other things. Education is one of those other things.

Enlightenment

True enlightenment is having knowledge and genuine understanding and then acting on that wisdom. But we are told that the ultimate enlightenment is having knowledge and understanding of the self and how the self fits into the world. There is a quote from Zen Buddhism that can be found in just about every book on enlightenment. It is: *"Before enlightenment, chop wood, carry water. After enlightenment, chop wood, carry water."* Not many of us chop wood or carry water today, but what it means is that no matter how enlightened you become, life has its daily duties and responsibilities. After enlightenment, you do those things with a slightly different mindset and intent. Finding your true self and true path is perhaps the genuine path of enlightenment. But it can't be obtained as long as your beliefs and feelings form the basis of your actions. The part of enlightenment that comes with understanding the world comes from accepting that all you truly control is what you do in the present moment, until there are no moments left.

Diligence & Decency

Diligence is making a continual and genuine effort to accomplish your goals and to fulfill your responsibilities. It relates to being careful in one's actions and to be persistent and consistent in behavior. Half-hearted trying, giving up, and being a victim get in the way of diligence. Focusing on having an easy life will lead you to seeking pleasure and avoiding pain, and that, in turn, leads to plenty of traps. So too does depriving others and being mean. Many times previously we have mentioned that most humans want to be better than they are. We believe that the majority of people want to lead noble, decent lives. Decency is a personal quality that implies a lot of characteristics. It implies wanting to do what's right and to not hurt others. Warren Buffet's earlier quote exemplifies why decency is smart. He stated that, "Honesty pays off; being a good, decent person usually leads to success in business." Arbesman (2012) cited research on the relationship between fundamental "niceness" and success by scientists. He related, "Nicer people are indeed more creative, more successful, and even more likely to win Nobel prizes." And being decent forms lasting and beneficial relationships. You can increase your chances of winning a Nobel prize by being nice.

Obligations, Observation, & Optimism

Life is filled with obligations. If you chose them, own them. Fulfill them and keep your agreements. Don't be deceptive or look for excuses to avoid obligations that you have committed to. If others choose obligations for you, take a good look at why you have accepted them. Learn from any mistakes you have made and don't repeat those same mistakes. Do the things you have to do, and do them with diligence and decency. Be careful not to become obligated to things that don't relate to your true path. At the same time, learn to become an observer in most things in life. Many situations should only be observed and learned from, rather than you actually becoming personally involved with them. The many examples we have cited about arguments ensuing over beliefs show how participating in these arguments leads to nowhere good or beneficial for either party. Learn to observe your own beliefs and feelings rather than allowing them to exert control over your actions and decisions. Doing this can allow you to become more optimistic. In a world full of pessimism, it can be difficult to become, and remain, optimistic. Being optimistic about your life bestows numerous potential benefits. There is clear evidence that having an optimistic outlook promotes a variety of health benefits. No one is certain about exactly why this is so, but heart disease and many other chronic illnesses tend to be present to a lesser extent in people who are optimistic.

Motivation

How successful you are in life depends on a number of things. Luck, being in the right place at the right time, possessing certain skills and abilities, the people you know, social connections, and lots of other things play roles in success. But the greatest and most important factor of success is you and your motivation. You either want things badly enough that you are motivated to get them, or you aren't and you don't get them. It is all about desire and willingness to do the things that it takes to make things happen in your life. You are in control of your motivation. Remember that we have an unconscious tendency to follow the path of least resistance. We inherently seek to lead easy lives. Being motivated is a conscious choice and takes some effort. You have to make that choice, or the unconscious forces that lead you to the path of least resistance and having an easy, unfulfilling life will take over.

Two (2) Selves

By now you should understand that we have been trying to convey that people have two selves. There is the self you are now, and the one you are striving to be—your True Self. In life, we are all striving to become superior—to be something more than we are right now. We believe that the ultimate form of striving for superiority manifests when a person discovers his or her true path. You won't find true happiness and satisfaction until you discover your true self and your true path. Remember, however, your true path doesn't imply that there is only one perfect job or one perfect career for you. It implies that there is probably a right way for you to live and conduct your life. The choices you make will determine whether or not you follow that path. Staying the way you are right now is easy. You are unconsciously wired to stay unchanged. And having an easier life is one of human's primary drives. Many people seem to prefer to live an unhappy, unfulfilling but easy life. If that's your goal, you won't have much motivation to change, and you'll find excuses to keep things as they are. Becoming who you really want to be, your superior self, is challenging, and accomplishing this requires willpower and commitment to making necessary changes in how you live your life.

Commitment

Commitments are agreements. These agreements can be made with others or you can make them with yourself. We have already said it, but we'll say it again. Keep your agreements; if you commit to something, do it—follow through. This relates to fundamental honesty. However, the most important commitments in life, perhaps other than caring for children and close relationships, are those you make to yourself. Commit yourself to become the best person you can be. Commit yourself to not be driven by unconscious forces.

Commit yourself to take control of what you do and the decisions you make. Commit yourself to being aware of your beliefs and feelings and how they influence your actions in the world you live in. When you break one of your commitments, or can't keep it, learn from it. Don't be complacent by just letting things happen. Commit to consistently moving forward on your path in life.

Honesty

Honesty is the underpinning of everything related to happiness and success. People lie. That's a basic truth in psychology, and chances are, you already know it. Lying conceals things. It conceals things we'd rather not face or admit to anyone. Let us be very clear, we aren't saying that anyone can become perfectly honest. "Perfect honesty" is likely a fictional goal. What we are saying is that the closer you get to honesty, the better your life will work. Lying can seem to make things easier in the moment, and once again, we are confronted with the idea that we are driven to live easier lives and to take the path of least resistance. But in the long run, lying creates a host of problems that will eventually have to be dealt with. In the long run, honesty pays off, just as Warren Buffett has stated.

Authenticity

Authenticity and genuineness are related but aren't precisely the same thing. And our use of the term relates to making your beliefs and feelings authentic. Many people know deep down that some of their beliefs are incorrect, misleading, only partly correct, or simply not true. They are also aware that the feelings attached to many of these beliefs are unhealthy and hurtful. You should look at your beliefs the same way you might look at documents. Documents are authenticated by examining them. They are real or not real; they reflect reality or they don't. There is another idea expressed by many others about living an authentic life. It means that what you do in life is fully in line with your values and priorities. One example of an inauthentic life might be the father who believes he values being a role model for his children, but he gets drunk on the weekends or is abusive.

An authentic life is consistently acting in ways that reflect your priorities. In order to be authentic, you have to really understand what you value and what your true priorities are. Then you have to live in accordance with them.

Nobleness

Several times throughout this book, we have stressed that most people desire to be better than they are and would like to lead a noble life. Nobleness is characterized by dignity, generosity, honor, and having high personal standards of conduct. Many of the most influential leaders in the world displayed characteristics of nobleness. One of the most important aspects in nobleness relates to the injustice that happens in the world. There is injustice and inequality in the world we live in. Inequality is built into life. People may be equal in the eyes of God and maybe in the eyes of the law, but the reality is that when people enter this world, they aren't all equal in a lot of ways. Some of the things that create instant inequities among us are: looks, intelligence, the background we are born into, and physical characteristics bestowed upon us from heredity. It is up to you to decide whether there is a mission for you in this, but we are all responsible for our own interactions in this fundamentally unjust world. The following sentence summarizes living a noble life, and it has been stated by a lot of people in a lot of ways: *"You should seek to live a just life in an unjust world."* That's nobility.

Genuineness

Genuineness is often misunderstood. For our purposes, we'll state it like this. It is actually being who and what you say you are. It means you act in accordance with your values, ideas about right and wrong, and your priorities. It means you don't violate your standards. As we have repeatedly said, in the quest to make an easier life for ourselves, we allow ourselves to slip. We fail to keep some agreements. We let our feelings and emotions drive us to do and say things that cause harm to others. We lie to cover things up. The way for you to show genuineness is by being consistent in the way you live your life.

Epiphany

Whether they know it or not, most people seek to have an epiphany in life. In his many talks, Alan Watts spoke about an epiphany as similar to waking up. It's a sudden insight and instant awareness about something of significant importance. In essence, an epiphany is when the reality of something truly important suddenly becomes clear—the true meaning usually manifests itself in a symbolic image or mental insight. Sometimes it comes in the form of a vision; other times it's a flash of insight. But it's always about something of importance.

Many spiritual leaders relate that we tend to go through life unaware, as if we are asleep. In this book we have mentioned that a great deal of what we do is automatic and takes little to no thought at all. It comes from our unconscious. We act like biological robots. The fundamental idea this book stresses is that we can wake up by looking at how our beliefs and feelings emerge automatically and are seldom challenged. In the 1997 movie *Grosse Pointe Blank*, epiphany was referred to as *Shakubuku*. It was described as, "a swift spiritual kick to the head that alters your reality forever." It doesn't happen to everyone, but when it does, it is life-changing. Some people who have near-death experiences relate that they had an epiphany after being declared clinically dead and then returning to life. It has also happened to many people when they became a parent and were then responsible for someone other than themselves. Epiphany experiences can also spontaneously come from highly stressful situations as well as from periods of meditation or prayer. An epiphany is a very personal event that has lasting effects. And such experiences are hoped for by many people when they feel life is out of control.

People who work in substance abuse treatment centers often encounter patients who ask God to send them a message. They want a lightning strike. We know a few of them who actually asked God to strike them with lightning and change them. What that means is they don't want to take responsibility for changing themselves. They want that decision to be made for them. They want to be forced to change. Still another issue is frequently encountered in such treatment centers. Clients engage in endless discussion and speculation trying to understand *why* they are the way they are. They try to search their past to seek out answers and ultimately find a reason or something else upon which they can place blame. "I just want to know why I am like this," they say. They don't really want to know the truth. They are the way they are because of choices they made. In such cases, it is often based in trying to live an easier life with more pleasure and avoiding pain and boredom. Drugs and alcohol promise an easy and pleasurable life—at least in the beginning. Then the trap springs. It always indicates that the person isn't on their true path, and that they have violated just about every characteristic found in this chapter. You can create a life-changing epiphany by confronting your own beliefs and the feelings attached to them.

CHAPTER 11

Common Pitfalls and Choices

There are countless situations that get in the way of finding a true path in life and countless decisions we make that restrict our freedom. This chapter will present some of the most common ones. It's not an all-inclusive list, but it does outline some of the key situations faced at different periods and stages of life.

Control of Others—Relationships and Entanglements

Far too many people say they are unhappy because of entanglements in relationships. The word "entanglements" implies efforts are being made to control issues involving other people that aren't under your control. As we have mentioned several times, you can't really control others, at least other people beyond their childhood years (even then it can be quite a chore). Older children and teenagers need to have guidance and you need to make efforts to have standards and rules with them; however, children and teenagers have minds of their own. Make your rules as fair and as understandable as possible, and enforce them with consequences established in advance. With adults, however, all you can do is have your own personal set of relationship guidelines and standards that are made clear. The issue with relationship entanglements often comes when you find that the other person isn't staying in line with the guidelines you have established—at least in accordance with the set of beliefs you have about the relationship. Entanglements also come from times you don't follow the guidelines. A common problem is that such guidelines have never been made clear or have not been openly communicated. However, if a relationship is abusive, it seldom resolves easily. It's recognized that there are a lot of people who move from one abusive relationship to another. If this is the case with you, we urge you to seek professional help.

Sometimes there are relationships that need to be ended. Ultimately, whether or not you feel it is time for you to end a relationship is up to you to determine. Keep in mind that there are only two things you truly control: your actions and your decisions. You control what you do right now, at this exact moment. So that moment is already over and you are in another. We are going to state this again in a slightly different way. You control what you do in the here-and-now, the ever-changing present moment. You control the decisions you make. What you put in your body and what your body does are nearly always under your control. And you will control what you choose to do in the future—all of the here-and-now moments that are coming. Yes, you do control some of your future, and every decision you make will have an effect on future situations and the decisions you will have to make.

The most nagging problems in life tend to come in our interactions with other people. We take part in important interactions with others, which stimulate change for both people. Both you and those with whom you interact will tend to be better or worse as a consequence of each interaction. You have to learn to engage with others without a hidden agenda—be genuine. Doing this makes you more influential as well as a better person. True power and influence comes from people being drawn to you because of what you are and how you are, not the position you hold. You can't have secret motives. Every interaction you have with another person has an impact—positive, negative, big, or small. Everything you do in secret has an impact. If people are made better by interacting with you, they will remember it. Life in our increasingly complex world needs simple truths. Our advice regarding how to deal with relationship issues is to go back and read the last half of the last chapter—Chapter 10. You should search out and examine your own behavior with respect to the list of important personal characteristics given in that chapter. The only thing you can control is you, so that's why we recommend you look at yourself. Keep in mind the qualities we believe to be important are: Freedom; Responsibility; Education; Enlightenment; Diligence & Decency; Obligations, Observations, & Optimism; Motivation; Two (2) Selves; Commitment; Honesty; Authenticity; Nobleness; Genuineness; and Epiphany.

Routines and Habits

Developing habits and routines in life is both necessary and smart. You probably have some bad habits, and you already know what they are. The same can be said for good habits; you also know what they are. Your habits and routines not only keep you in the flow of your life, but they set up what may happen in your future and express some of the essence of your identity. One of the areas of habits we will briefly discuss is health. Health is perhaps the most important area in your life because it exerts a profound influence over everything you do. The things you put into your body and how you treat your body now have the power to affect your future health and freedom. Eating junk food or fast food because it is easier forms bad eating habits. Not exercising or not being active because it takes effort can lead to lazy habits. Habits (like not exercising) can give you freedom now, but they can also restrict your future freedom if you have made poor decisions. One of the things you should do is conduct an overall assessment of your habits, both good and bad, and look at them realistically. Look at the things you routinely do, how you spend your time, the types of conversations you have, and the people, places, and things in your life, and assess them. You'll see things that you can, and should, improve. Think of this process like running yourself through a sieve to remove the bad stuff. You can do this again and again to refine your life.

Chained to the Digital and Social Media Age

If you have teenagers or are below the age of 40, chances are pretty good that you are somehow chained to social media and digital devices. If you keep your primary digital device near you at all times, you are in essence chained to it. We can't say that staying connected is a bad thing in and of itself. Then again, there are some really negative aspects involved with the age of social media. Currently, there is increasing discussion of "addiction" to social media and digital devices. While such an idea may seem radical, it is probably pretty accurate for many people. Research has shown that the same brain areas involved in addiction to drugs are involved with interactions on social media. "Likes," "shares," and message notifications produce the same instant rush of brain chemicals that drug use does (Soat, 2015). In addition, nearly everyone knows that the influence celebrities have with society is far too great. Celebrities typically lead a lifestyle that is appealing to the masses. Our ideas of ideal men and women are today being formed by internet videos of individuals "breaking the internet" with selfies and videos of themselves showing skin, partying, or just showing off material things. What do you think is motivating the person who claims he or she had a video go "viral" or "broke the internet?" Too many young people see images of beautiful people that have been altered to make them more attractive, more "perfect." It creates a false image of normality and a fictional image of what life is about. In the digital world, self-esteem comes from getting "likes" or from our number of "friends" or followers. People feel pressured to share and "like" everyone's posts. If you think that the influence of all of this will cease or decline in the future, you are probably wrong. It will likely transform, but will not go away.

Alan Watts, who died in 1973, long before the digital age existed, had some prophetic words about it. Back then, he was discussing how everyone was being forced to document their activities at work, to cover themselves and ultimately their employers from potential liability. He stated, "It's become more important to record what you do rather than do what you do." Today, people record the meals they eat, what they drink, the places they go, their various daily activities, and themselves, over and over with endless selfies. We have become more than obsessed with ourselves. We want to share ourselves with others who we call friends in what may be an effort to show everyone what a great a life we lead. Related to this discussion is a term you probably have never heard. It is *Dunbar's Number*.

Back in 1992, anthropologist Robin Dunbar decided to determine a human's true capacity for having meaningful relationships. Dunbar's Number is the number of people we can have genuine, meaningful social ties with at any one time. He calculated that we could have about 150 such relationships, give or take another 50 or so (Dunbar, 1992). Some other researchers have since calculated that the number varies from 50 to just under 300. You have probably gathered a lot more social media "friends" than that. But many of them are friends purely in a "click" sense, meaning that they will "like" some of your posts from time to time. These are people you don't speak with very often, if ever. You have a genuine relationship with far fewer people. Social media gives us the illusion of being connected to lots of people. Exactly what this will mean in the future isn't known. But it's likely that many of our future relationships will be primarily "virtual" relationships. We will probably experience less face-to-face interaction and with fewer people.

If you have children, it's more than a good idea to restrict their use of digital devices. Get them outside and teach them how to play, use their imagination, and appreciate nature. Put the phones and devices away for planned periods of time. There is an increasing trend in which we are allowing children to live in virtual worlds when they are indoors and we are not encouraging them to learn about reality and relationships. Far too many parents encourage their children to play with digital devices so that their children are occupied and "out of the way." This all has consequences, and the consequences play a huge role in how well children will adapt to the real world later in life. It also plays a huge role in their ability to socialize with others on a personal level.

There is also increasing evidence that certain video games may promote violent behavior. There is no doubt that an obsession to gaming can occur and it becomes so strong that it displays all the characteristics of addiction. In the gaming world, players kill thousands of others without any consequences. How much does this influence their beliefs and feelings? No one really knows for certain. But we do know it does have an effect. Everything we do has an effect. The digital world is going to create even bigger problems in the coming years as virtual devices become readily available that can easily access sexual content. If you have children, this is something you will have to recognize, educate them about, and protect them from. But the same can be said for most of us, no matter one's age. What do you think the consequences might be if you could have what will feel like real sex with anyone you choose in a virtual world? How could this affect your intimate relationships with real people?

Money

You can't buy happiness with money, at least that's the old adage. You can certainly have less stress with financial security, but true happiness comes from more than money. Buying things never leads to lasting happiness and can actually lead to endless buying. Buying things can lead to the same brain chemical rush that comes from drugs, but it's temporary, as is everything. The truth is that happiness is a state of being and state of mind that ebbs and wanes. Once you meet your basic needs, your happiness is up to you, not money. Most people greatly overestimate the extent to which money relates to happiness. We always adjust to having more money and it often leads to seeking even more money. Getting stuff doesn't create long-term satisfaction; it often leads to wanting more stuff. A recent study in the psychology journal *Emotion* (Piff & Moskowitz, 2017) evaluated factors related to happiness in over 1,500 Americans based on their income levels. The core factors they tell us that correlate to true happiness are amusement, a sense of awe, compassion, contentment, enthusiasm, love, and pride. Higher income and higher social class has long been linked to better health and higher levels of reported satisfaction in life, but not necessarily with happiness. What they found is that the higher income levels reported more pride, contentment, and amusement in life. Lower income levels showed greater levels of compassion, love, and feelings of awe. They concluded that those people who formed meaningful relationships laid the groundwork for greater happiness and contentment in life. Having real relationships and sharing life with other people important to you is far more conducive to happiness than money. But money can provide a sense of security.

Work and Career

This book has stressed making your work and career harmonious with your true path. You decide who and what you want to be (your true self), and your work and career will reflect those characteristics (a true path). As we mentioned before, many people seem to prefer to live an unhappy but easy life. If that's your goal, you won't have much motivation to change, and you'll find excuses to keep things as they are. You won't have to dig very deep for any excuses—they'll bubble up from the unconscious. The path of least resistance seldom involves making a change.

In general, if you find your true path in work, people will be drawn to you. You become more important by engaging in other people's interests and their lives—sometimes to a greater extent than with your own. That, of course, can go too far. But sharing with others and engaging with them is the key. People will be drawn to you for one of two reasons. One is what you can do or have already done for them. The other is what you are—who you are—and how you are. If you are honest and trustworthy, people will be drawn to you. You have to become genuinely interested in other people and their lives. If your work and career is unsatisfying, you have to assess that situation. Look at the options and possibilities that exist for you to make a change. Sometimes you have to have a willingness to start over.

Condemnation

Dale Carnegie taught some simple truths about how to conduct oneself at work, and these truths remain as relevant today as they have ever been (Carnegie, 2011). He stressed that we should refrain from criticism and condemnation of others. Don't make complaints about someone unless it's something that really matters. And make such complaints only in the spirit of genuine concern that recognizes the difficulty that others have. In graduate school, one of authors was intrigued by the physiologist Hans Selye, who was best known as being the originator of the *General Adaptation Syndrome*. Basically it refers to our physiological reactions to stress. Selye has been widely quoted as saying, "As much as we thirst for approval, we dread condemnation." Condemnation causes a psychological resistance and calling it psychological here doesn't mean it's just in the mind or our thoughts. We *feel* condemnation physically. It produces a biochemical reaction in the brain. Areas of the brain are engaged when we are being criticized or condemned. Years ago Greg conducted some professional trainings in a very confrontational way. That was a mistake. It provoked strong reactions in the group of professionals being trained, and what it did was make many of the people actively look for ways to retaliate, to find fault, or argue. So, before engaging in arguments or confrontational complaining, take some time to quiet down the physiological components that are unconscious. Learn how to soften your messages.

Enemies

Chances are that somewhere lurking within your sphere of life, you believe you have some enemies. These are people who want you to fail, want what you want in a competitive way, simply don't like you, or are seen as an obstacle in your path. That happens in our competitive world; it always has; and it always will. There is an old saying: "Misery loves company." For some unhappy people who feel like their life is miserable, they appear to be consoled by the failure of others.

An example of the phenomenon of enemies comes in work environments, in any groups you might participate, and even in families. How it's typically described is like this: "Things here would be great if [insert that person's name] wasn't around." Sometimes it's true. But more often than not, someone else would rise to the occasion and assume that role. A really good way to evaluate our perceived enemies and others who present barriers to us is to use them to learn about ourselves and find success by going around them. Determine precisely what it is that the person does that is irritating to us and creates issues. There is a good chance that some aspect of that person is something that you have been fighting within yourself. Sometimes you can directly ask questions of them, such as, "Exactly what are you wanting to get out of this?" Then listen. Avoid arguing and confrontation, and just listen. Resistance is a two-way street. It takes at least two people to have an argument. A good strategy is to give the other person room and time to say all that they have to say. Eventually, they'll hear themselves speaking and repeating the same message, again and again. Let them run down by allowing them to repeat themselves and sooner or later they will probably cease talking. If the other person is a true enemy, sometimes all you can do is go around them and squeeze them out of having influence on you. The very fact that you might see someone as an enemy implies that they have some sort of influence on you. Again, you have to remember that the only thing you really control is you and what you do in the present moment.

Here is a real situation where a woman (we will call Elizabeth) felt she had an enemy at work. Elizabeth was a friendly person, worked very hard, and was a quick learner. She even offered to do extra work when she was finished with her assigned duties. She was new to a job, and a coworker soon befriended her—but eventually Elizabeth realized that she was not really a friend. The coworker would take Elizabeth's ideas to their boss as if they were her own and was credited publicly with some of these "great ideas." Elizabeth also found out that the coworker was talking badly about her to others in the office. Initially, Elizabeth was very hurt and became withdrawn at work. But as time went on, she realized that her coworker was jealous of her and that the jealous behavior was not going to change. Elizabeth could have stewed with angry feelings or responded in kind and spread rumors about the coworker, but instead she decided to be herself, keep working as she was, and not tell the coworker any of her ideas anymore. The coworker did not stop spreading rumors, but the rest of the office staff soon realized what kind of person Elizabeth was by her actions. Some even told Elizabeth they told the coworker to stop coming to them with negativity. A couple years later, the gig was up and the coworker left for a different job. Elizabeth was promoted shortly thereafter. Elizabeth had a lot of beliefs and feelings about the coworker, and it affected her personality at work for a short time. However, by deciding to ignore her feelings about the coworker, she squeezed the coworker out of having influence over her and profited in the end.

Health and Habits

We have mentioned health many times, but it is such an important issue we'll address it again. Health is one of those areas where far too many people shirk personal responsibility. Today it's common knowledge that what you eat, drink, and your physical activity levels are directly related to your health. You probably know many facts about this, but how difficult is it for most people to take a few walks each day? Studies have shown us that certain foods and drinks are unhealthy. You know that's true. The main issue that impedes us is a fact that has been mentioned many times here. We strive to lead easier lives. We seek pleasure in the moment. All the reasons to not change things bubble up automatically from the unconscious. We put off doing healthy things until tomorrow, because it's inconvenient today, or we want to take it easy and enjoy ourselves today. But each day has a new tomorrow on the horizon, so it's put off again and the cycle continues.

One more unpleasant piece of information is important to cite here. There is a very good chance that your path to death—or health problems later in life—have been put in motion by the habits you have already formed. There are strong genetic issues that relate to our health, but what we do and what we consume has a strong influence on our health, especially when underlying issues start to emerge. What you do and the choices you make are the part you control. You choose one way or the other. Even if you don't think you are actively making a choice, you are in effect *choosing* to do nothing and to keep your health the way it currently is and on the path it's heading down. However, you should accept that your behavior does have a very real impact on your health—for better or worse.

The Inevitability of Aging

If you live long enough, you'll get old. Of course it's a trite statement, but it's still true. We are supposedly the only creatures with the knowledge that we are aging and going to die. For young people, it seems absurd or unnecessary to plan for old age. The future is unpredictable, right? But doing the things that facilitate health isn't absurd or unnecessary. When you are young, you think you are immune to ill health, or you say something we have heard countless times in treatment centers: "I'll cross that bridge when I come to it." We might ask, "What will happen if your behavior gets you fired?" They say, "I'll cross that bridge when I come to it." "What if you don't save enough for retirement?" Same answer. "What if this gets you hurt or sick?" Same answer. Okay. We can't control everything. But what we do now produces later choice points. There are future consequences to our present and past decisions. Lots of people avoid going to the doctor because they don't want to know if something is wrong. So, how does this relate to age? We just said it. What we do now produces later choice points. Our future choices can get really restricted by nagging health issues or poor financial decisions until there are no desirable options left. If you are older, and it's up to you to decide what "older" might mean, you still need to have a purpose in life. You still have a true path. It might be volunteering for a cause. It might be serving as a mentor. It's up to you. But if you are approaching some crucial points in life, like nearing retirement, or you can see frailty creeping up on you, what you do now has genuine implications and significance.

In the medical area of geriatrics and senior care, the idea of *morbidity compression* has become rather influential. This concept was first proposed around 1980 by James Fries of Stanford University. It is the now-accepted idea that all the illnesses associated with old age can be compressed into a relatively short period before death. That is, the medical community believes that chronic and serious health issues should be kept at bay as long as possible. It keeps the quality of life high and reduces costs to individuals, families, and whatever social structure has to bear the burden. It's also a way to minimize the effects of aging and illness on those around us. The theory of morbidity compression also asserts that all of the health issues we have been managing or keeping at bay with medications or therapy, will one day catch up with us. They all tend to hit at once and with a vengeance at the end. You want to minimize the time frame at "the end" as much as possible. At least that's the idea.

You can let life's circumstances control you, or you can take some control over your life. It is often a human tendency to wait until something bad happens before we take action. And at that point, it can be too late. We seek certainty and there isn't much of that in later life. The only certainty is that it's going to end. Related to this idea is a concept stressed by senior living experts. They say, "It is better to prepare than repair." It means exactly what it says. If you are nearing your later years, you can, and should, prepare. Consider where you can, or will, live. Think about who can, or will, take care of the things you won't be able to do. Something we have all heard from aging parents is, "I want to stay in my house as long as I can." That's normal and certainly understandable. But it can place a burden on those who are around before and when we depart. It's something worth thinking deeply about and discussing with those who will bear your burden. If you actually talk to people who transitioned from their home to a senior living center, many of them will tell you the same thing. That is, they were unsure about it at first, but it was the smartest thing they ever did.

Failure

We have all failed at something. No matter how hard you try, you will fail at something. Your children will fail in some of their attempts at doing new things. Failure is an inevitable consequence of trying. Trying can sometimes be so demoralizing that we just stop trying, and that is failure. Think about how we earlier described some of the drug users in treatment. They "quit" using drugs many times. Some of them simply stopped trying to quit. But there are lots and lots of *former* drug users and *former* alcoholics. They quit and stayed quit. What was their secret? They quit and they stayed quit. They made choices about their actions and kept their agreements. They learned from their mistakes. They didn't give up. Resilience is the ability to learn from failure. Real failure is when you stop trying—when you give up. Resilience isn't self-condemning. Resilience is about personal growth and developing internal strength. Learning from our failures is a way we can bring out the best in ourselves. It makes us stronger through repeated practice. So make it safe for yourself to fail and for others to fail, and call it practice. Provide a safe place to "try" things and encourage yourself to try without the fear of failure as a factor.

The issue of failure ends this chapter because it is the fear of failure that is one of the big barriers that stands in the way of making real change. Making a commitment to change brings up the possibility of failure. Fear of failure stops us from learning and keeps us from trying until we succeed. At that point it becomes easy to just keep things as they are—to follow the path of least resistance. So as a simple example, let's imagine that you are shy or uncomfortable interacting with others and that it's something you want to change. If you see yourself as shy, you'll purposefully avoid interacting with others. You typically avoid others and then you don't experience the discomfort of interacting with others, which in turn reinforces your shyness. In brief, the more a person acts shy, the stronger their shyness gets. Just like any superstitious behavior, the more the behavior is repeated, the stronger the belief about the behavior becomes.

What you need to do is directly confront such self-limiting beliefs by doing or practicing the exact opposite of them. If you are shy and want that to change, act as if you aren't shy. When the opportunity presents itself, make it a point to talk to people you don't know. Do this again and again. The failure will only come if you stop trying and stop practicing the opposite behaviors of shyness. If you want to be healthier, act as if you are healthy. How? Do the things that healthy people do. Increase your activity level; eat healthy foods; avoid bad habits; and go to the doctor for regular check-ups. Healthy people tend to visit doctors regularly. If you are angry and react emotionally to things, act as if you are happy and calm. Control your outer reactions. The more you let anger and emotion out, the more it'll come out. Practice acting the way you want to be. Failure is okay as long as you don't stop trying. If you keep practicing, the failed attempts will only be temporary. In essence, what we are encouraging you to do is to make a commitment. Commit yourself to make an effort to bring out the best in yourself and others. You know what your problem areas are. Take responsibility for them and make the effort to change them.

CHAPTER

Seeing Life as a Game

We have mentioned the concept of life being a game a few times previously. Up until now we have avoided addressing this concept because the term "game" has the potential to trivialize life. Of course, a lot of life's aspects can seem like a game. There are endless scenarios that could be viewed as "competitions" in life. Life is filled with rules and laws. There are unwritten rules related to sportsmanship, fairness, and how we should treat others. There are penalties for violating the rules. Some people get away with cheating; some people are caught. Some people are accused of cheating even when they haven't done so. Society certainly does identify some people as winners or losers in life. But let's make it clear that if life is a game, it's a serious game, and one with very high stakes. There are consequences to everything we do. And this life may well be the only time we play. You can believe what you want about that, but perhaps we can say it a more palatable way. We think that you should treat this life as if it will be the only one you'll have. If you have an "afterlife," that's a whole different life.

There are a number of rules that have been made about the game, rules we have to follow. Few of us made the rules, but we still have to follow them or face some consequences. The rules can be complicated and can be different in different places and under different circumstances. The rules in Egypt are different than they are in America. The rules can, and do, change suddenly. People bend the rules. Sometimes they get caught, sometimes they don't. The rules and requirements of the game are a bit different at different stages of life. The rules for young children are different than they are for teens.

The rules for parents are different than those of older adults without children. The game also changes as one reaches later stages of life.

There are various ideologies, "coaching methods," and life-change workshops that have long claimed that life is a game. One of the fundamental ideas many of these approaches assert is that the primary goal of the game of life is to survive. We have mentioned previously that humans do have a fundamental drive to survive. And you'll survive until you don't survive. You have quite a bit of control over how long you'll survive, but ultimately, no one gets out alive. No one survives indefinitely. It's pretty simple.

The whole idea of survival is at the bottom of Maslow's hierarchy of needs. Survival is as basic as it gets. In the modern world, survival has become much easier than it ever has been. People live longer today than they did just 10 years ago. Keep going back in time and you will find that the average lifespan was shorter and shorter. When we were hunter-gatherers many thousands of years ago, life was almost solely about individual survival—and survival of the human race. But things change as we have stated repeatedly, and today the "game" of life isn't really about survival. If you play the game to survive and win, you never get any higher on Maslow's hierarchy of needs. *The real issue is what you do in life while you survive.* You might see it like you are in competition with others, but the only genuine competition takes place within you. So let's run with this idea of life as a game.

We assert that the game of life is about finding your true self and your true path. You give your life whatever meaning it has through the things you do and the effect you have on others. But as long as you exist, you'll have to be a part of the game. Even if you are alone, you are in the game. Your game of life can be played alone, with just a few people, or with a lot of people.

There are two basic ways to engage in the game. One way is to see it as a competition. This will imply that there are winners and losers, and for some people winning is everything. Conflicts, hurt feelings, condemnation of others, accusations, and hurtful behavior stems from seeing it as a competition. Playing it as a competition can, and often does, lead to developing the opposite of all of the personality characteristics previously described as central to finding one's true path. When the game is played as a competition *against* others, almost everyone loses, whether they are aware of it or not.

On the other hand, the game can be seen more like a round of golf. Only a small percentage of people reading this play golf, and what most people think about golf has probably been influenced by tournaments they have watched and reports by the media. There are reasons why a lot of older people play the game of golf. For most, it's about being with other people, being engaged in a pleasant activity outside, and simply doing the best you can with the resources you have. People who play golf tend to try to just do the best they can with the ability and skill that they possess. If it's a competition, it's most often a personal competition with yourself, trying to get a little better. People who aren't good at playing golf even get an adjustment in their score if they are playing in some sort of competition. But even those "competitions" are more about having fun, being outside, and being with others rather than winning. Again, it's just trying to do the best you can and get a little better at it while having fun. We see this as the way to play life's game, if that's what it is. You do the best you can with the resources available to you. You try to get better and you practice. You have fun with others while you do it and you don't take the competition aspect all that seriously. In golf, no one has ever shot a "perfect score" and such a concept doesn't even exist in golf. A "round" of golf is playing 18 holes, and a perfect score would be 18, meaning you hit the ball in each hole with one and only one swing. It's never been done except in putt-putt golf. And it wouldn't be much fun if you did that every time you played. You will not be perfect in life, either. You will make mistakes, but learn from those mistakes and practice becoming better at the game. Share your experience(s) with others so that they can learn, and listen to their experiences so that you can learn.

Mindfulness

In recent years the Zen idea of mindfulness has found a firm footing in psychological treatment. Mindfulness is ultimately about being in the moment, being aware of each moment. That's all you have anyway, as we have previously stated. Mindfulness relates to not focusing on the past or what is coming in your future, it's about the here-and-now. That's what this book has been about. We have stressed that all you control is what you do right now. The things we have called unconscious influences are stemming from the past. Your beliefs are primarily about the past. All you have is now. There are countless audio resources available to people to practice mindfulness techniques, and just about all of them can be helpful. The basic concept is usually just relaxing, focusing on your breathing, and trying to totally clear your mind and focus on being alive. Other mindfulness techniques include completely focusing on an object— eliminating all other thoughts and just experiencing the thing you are focusing on. It can be a flower, a tree, a bird, a pencil—it doesn't matter. The purpose is to completely focus on what is in the here-and-now and not get distracted by thoughts of the past or the future.

How Will I Use This Day?

In the Paul "Bear" Bryant Museum at the University of Alabama is a piece of well-worn paper the famous coach carried around in his wallet. He supposedly pulled it out each day and read it, and he was known to read it regularly to his teams. It was a prayer written by a Texas accountant and motivational speaker, Heartsill Wilson. Here are some excerpts from it:

> *"This is the beginning of a new day. ... I can waste it or use it for good. ... When tomorrow comes, this day will be gone forever, leaving something in its place... I want it to be gain, not loss—good, not evil."*

The poem is an apt reminder for us to seize the day, to use the time we have in life and put it to good use. Maybe that's all life asks of us. Maybe we just go around life one time. Maybe we don't. You can believe whatever you want about this, but it doesn't matter what you believe right now. You will either know someday that you have an afterlife, or you'll just disappear and cease to exist, perhaps like you did in the roughly 10 billion years of the universe's existence before you came along. All that matters right now, is now. That's all you have. Choose how you will live and how you will treat others. If you believe that some religious ideology is the key, seize it. If you reject it all, you'll still be here—until you aren't. What you are doing in each moment is all there is—there is nothing else. The final thing we will repeat here at the end is pretty simple, so simple it's really all you need to know. You have to treat this life as if it's the only life you will ever have.

Self-Coaching

There are many possible reasons people read self-help books. However, it's likely that there is a common and simple thread running through those reasons. People are trying to improve some areas of their lives. They want to change something for the better.

In some cases, there are deep-seated problems and issues that require professional help. But perhaps the vast majority of people who read self-help books want to cope with their issues on their own or without engaging in formal counseling or therapy. In recent years the idea of "life-coaching" has caught on, and it can be a useful endeavor for many who are seeking assistance. Life-coaching has various definitions but all of them imply that the person seeking to improve his or her life gets assistance from another who gives some guidance and mentoring. If you need professional help, we urge you to seek out someone qualified for whatever your needs may be. If you are seeking a life coach, there are a lot of them out there. However, there are many people who want to deal with their issues in their own ways, without involving a professional. We suggest you think of this as "self-coaching."

There are quite a few books about self-coaching, most of which concern controlling or changing some sort of pathology, but here we want to present it in a different way. Coaching always implies encouragement, support, and guidance from another who supposedly has more experience and expertise in whatever it is that is being sought. So the important question to start with is, "Who provides the encouragement, support, and guidance in self-coaching?"

The answer to this question has been mentioned many times in this book, but chances are that "our answer" won't come to mind immediately. Of course you will probably immediately think that with "self-coaching" the answer is you. That's true, at least in an obvious but not precisely accurate way. But that's not our final answer.

The main title of this book is *Freedom To Change*, and in Chapter 10 we called it Freedom 2 Change. Do you recall what the number "2" refers to? It is on page 131. That is our answer.

Many times in this book we have mentioned the idea that we all have two selves. These two selves are *the person we are now* and *the person we are trying to be*. Many of the ideas we have discussed relate to our two selves including Maslow's theory, the concept of striving for superiority, and various others. We have also addressed the concepts of a True Path and a True Self. *In self-coaching, the person you are now is coached and encouraged by the person you are striving to be.* There is a good chance that the person you are striving to be has high standards, good habits, and has the positive personality and behavioral characteristics we mentioned in Chapter 10. So, in the simplest way possible, you let the standards of your "aspiring true self" be your coach and mentor. If you can embrace this idea, you'll find it quite useful. One thing you can do when facing some situations is to ask yourself a simple question: What would my true self—my higher self—ask me to do? There are a lot of other ways you can phrase that question. For example, when faced with a decision you could ask, "If I really was the person I am trying to be, what would I do?"

Self-coaching requires you to set some goals and keep in mind that what you are doing is trying to become better than you are right now. Then, of course, you have to act in accordance with the ideals and goals you are aspiring to achieve. If you are consistent in keeping to this simple method, you should find yourself making progress. Keep at it long enough, and your true path will often just appear in front of you. But if your desire is to change something in your life, you have to do something different.

There are many famous quotes that relate this idea in their own way, and one of those interesting and relevant quotes came from a 2012 movie entitled, *The Samaritan*. It stated, "If you keep on doing what you've always done, you'll keep on being what you've always been."

Things To Keep In Mind—A Summary

There are several things you can do to change in the ways you desire, and practicing—or acting in the ways you want to be—is just one method. You also need to set some goals and challenge your beliefs about them. Remember that feelings are attached to beliefs and that beliefs don't always reflect True Truth. Try to follow the two big rules: Do no harm & do the best you can with the resources available to you. Also keep in mind that you are a creation and can change just about everything in your life if you want. But it's best to start with small, measurable goals. Failure only comes when you stop trying. The main obstacles come from a basic tendency buried in our unconscious. That is, we avoid unpleasant things and are generally wired to follow the path of least resistance. Finally, practice using the ABCD method. The more you practice, the easier it gets.

Thank you for reading. If we have helped you in any way, please post a review on Amazon and tell us how!

You can find video resources and additional program materials available for individuals and life coaches on our website:

www.freedom2change.org

REFERENCES

Arbesman, S. (2102) *The Half-Life of Facts*. NY: Penguin Books.

Atwood, M. (2017) True Truth.
http://www.swimbikemom.com/2017/02/truth-truth.html?doing_wp_cron=
1528749972.1117560863494873046875

Careerbuilder.com (2017) Living Paycheck to Paycheck is a Way of Life for Majority
of U.S. Workers, According to New Career Builder Survey. http://press.
careerbuilder.com/2017-08-24-Living-Paycheck-to-Paycheck-is-a-Way-of-
Life-for-Majority-of-U-S-Workers-According-to-New-CareerBuilder-Survey

Carnegie, D. (2011) *How to win friends & influence people in the digital age*.
NY: Simon & Schuster.

Cooper, R. (2013) First, do no harm?
http://eprints.lancs.ac.uk/76424/1/octrevisedpppapercleanversion.pdf

Dunbar, R. (1992) Neocortex size as a constraint on group size in primates.
Journal of Human Evolution, 22 (6), 469-493.

Elkins, K. (2017) Warren Buffett's best advice for young people has nothing to do
with business. https://www.cnbc.com/2017/01/30/warren-buffetts-best-
advice-for-young-people.html

Ellis, A. (1957) Rational psychotherapy and individual psychology.
Journal of individual psychology, 13, 38-44.

Givens, W. (2003) *Ninety-Nine Iron*. Tuscaloosa, AL: University of Alabama Press.

Hagura, N., Haggard, P., & Diedrichsen, J. (2017) Perceptual decisions are biased
by the cost to act. *eLife*, 2017;6:e18422.

Hardy, A. (2006) First do no harm. *EMBO Reports*, 7:12, 1199. Harvard Health
Publishing (2008) Optimism and your health. https://www.health.harvard.
edu/heart-health/optimism-and-your-health

Herbert, J., & Sageman, M. (2008) First do no harm.
https://onlinelibrary.wiley.com/doi/bs/10.1002/9780470713570.ch11

Introduction to Psychology (2017) Is personality more nature or more nurture?
Behavioral and molecular genetics. http://open.lib.umn.edu/intropsyc/
chapter/11-3-is-personality-more-nature-or-more-nurture-behavioral-and-
molecular-genetics/

Kahneman, D. (2011) Bias, blindness, and how we really think. *Bloomberg.com*.
Three-part article published October 24, 25, & 27, 2011.

Little, G. L. (1997) *Psychopharmacology: Basics for counselors*. Memphis: Advanced
Training Associates, LLC.

Little, G. L., (1997) *Staying Quit.* Memphis: ATA, LLC.

Little, G. L., Robinson, K. D., & Burnette, K. D. (1998) *Effective counseling approaches for chemical abusers & offenders.* Memphis: Eagle Wing Books, Inc.

Maslow, A. (1943) A theory of human motivation. *Psychological Review,* 50, 370-396.

McQueeney, R. (2017) Warren Buffett's advice to young people: Be a good person. https://www.zacks.com/stock/news/268156/warren-buffetts-advice-to-young-people-be-a-good-person

Peck, M. Scott. (1978) *The Road Less Traveled.* NY: Simon & Schuster.

Piff, P., & Moskowitz, J. (2017) Wealth, poverty, and happiness: Social class is differentially associated with positive emotions. *Emotion,* December 18: dx.doi.org/10.1037/emo0000378.

Rogers, C. (1951) *Client centered therapy.* London: Constable.

Saban, N. (2013) Check-in speech given by Nick Saban at NFSC 2013. YouTube.

Schwantes, M. (2018) Warren Buffett Says Integrity Is the Most Important Trait to Hire For. https://www.inc.com/marcel-schwantes/first-90-days-warren-buffetts-advice-for-hiring-based-on-3-traits.html

Soat, M. (2015) Social media triggers a dopamine high. *Marketing News,* November, 2015.

Soon, C., Brass, M., Heinze, H., & Haynes, J. (2008) Unconscious determinants of free decisions in the human brain. *Nature Neuroscience,* 11, 543-545.

Wanis, P. (2017) Can feelings be wrong? *Success Newsletter,* May 19. https://www.patrickwanis.com/can-feelings-be-wrong/

Watts, A. This is why you're not happy. www.youtube.com/watch?v=6Qb5sx65kRE

Webster, L. (2017) The Tribune was wrong. Medicine often involves a risk to the patient. http://thepainfultruthbook.com/2017/12/first-do-no-harm/

INDEX

ABOUT THE AUTHORS

Dr. Greg Little has a B.A. and M.S. in Psychology and an Ed.D. in Counseling & Educational Psychology from Memphis State University (now the University of Memphis). He is a retired LPC, a Nationally Certified Psychologist, and a Certified Life-Coach. His treatment programs for criminal personality, substance abuse, trauma, and Veterans are in use in all 50 states and in 9 countries. Over 3 million of his books are in print. He has authored or coauthored over 50 books and has been featured in 15 documentaries.

Kimberly Prachniak obtained her B.A. in Psychology from Sewanee and her M.S. in Community Agency Counseling from the University of Memphis. She worked previously as a drug and alcohol counselor at prisons in Memphis and as a corporate trainer, training other professionals across the U.S. and Canada in the rehabilitation of clients who were incarcerated or on parole. She currently serves as a Board member of a research review committee charged with aiding researchers in the protection of human subjects, and she is the Associate Director of that department where she has worked for over 10 years at a local university.

Stanley Prachniak received his B.A. in Psychology from the University of Memphis in 1999. In 2015, after serving several years in an upper-level management role, he made the decision to pursue a Master's degree in Business Administration. In 2018, he graduated with an M.B.A. from the University of Memphis. Upon graduation he released his first book *Getting a Job: And Exploring Career Possibilities*, which was developed to encourage juveniles and young adults to follow their interests when considering jobs and a career path. Stan's decision to return to school at the age of 41 allowed him to discover possibilities he had never considered before. He finally accepted that he had the power to change his life and become something better than he was. That is what *Freedom to Change* is all about.

Made in United States
Troutdale, OR
09/28/2024